UNLEASH YOUR HIDDEN POWERS

UNLEASH YOUR HIDDEN POWERS

SUHANI SHAH

JAICO PUBLISHING HOUSE

Ahmedabad Bangalore Chennai
Delhi Hyderabad Kolkata Mumbai

Published by Jaico Publishing House
A-2 Jash Chambers, 7-A Sir Phirozshah Mehta Road
Fort, Mumbai - 400 001
jaicopub@jaicobooks.com
www.jaicobooks.com

UNLEASH YOUR HIDDEN POWERS
ISBN 81-7992-670-2

First Jaico Impression: 2007
Fourth Jaico Impression: 2010

Printed by
Trinity Academy For Corporate Training Limited, Mumbai

Contents

Preface

When a child is born, he is sweet and innocent. The mind and physique of every newborn child is similar. Gradually, as the child grows up, physical and mental changes take place. Physical development is important but my aim in writing this book concerns the proper development of the mind. If the roots are not strong, even a light storm can uproot the tree. Therefore, understanding a child's mind and giving him proper guidance at the proper time is very necessary so that the child gets the right platform to develop.

Time keeps changing, the lifestyle of people in the 17th century was not as it was in the 15th century. You can easily differentiate between the standard of living in the 17th century and that of the 19th. After the 19th century, extreme changes have taken place. Now, we are living in the 21st century and so, we need to accept the definitions of this century and continually adapt ourselves to the changing conditions.

When we think about today's children, we can see that they have a lot of talent, but they are not able to realize it and the ones who do realize it, may not be able to select the right path. The definition of childhood has changed. These days, childhood is not a time to play and waste time. It should, instead, be utilized by the child for his betterment.

This is the time when, along with his school and college education, a person requires additional knowledge that could improve his mental abilities and help him to move ahead in life.

I am just 15 years old, and the main objective behind writing this book is to make each human being, whether younger or older than me, realize and understand that getting good marks in school or college or having a big business empire, is not enough to make you a successful person. You need to understand many subtle facts to live a proper life. If you try to understand these, then you can make yourself more confident and happy. Left to yourself, you may not be able to decide what is right for you and what is not. I have written this book, mainly for young people, so that they can understand the true value of their life and proceed towards a better way of living. However, any person who goes through this book will definitely understand the power of his mind and the abilities that are hidden within him. He will surely make himself better than he presently is.

I, being a magician, have been to many cities, states and countries and have observed different people. I have seen various people facing a wide range of problems which arise from a lack of understanding and knowledge. This is true even for highly educated people. Many people even come to me to share their problems, thinking that I will solve them by magic. Well, of course I cannot do that, as magic is just a trick and an art of presentation, not reality. However, since I played the role of a counselor, reading people's minds, understanding them and giving them proper answers became my duty. I sent them back satisfied, but at some point while I was observing such people, I thought it necessary to put down my views in black and white in the hope that they would help a larger number of people. The result is here in the form of this book.

I have written every topic of this book with complete concentration and honesty. Some might agree with my views and some may disagree, but I am confident enough to explain each point in a perfectly satisfying way. I have tried my level best to be very clear and to explain each detail in the most effective manner.

Suhani Shah

Introduction

As the title of the book suggests, this book is all about realizing and understanding that everyone in this world is complete. All one needs is to realize his inner abilities about which he is totally unaware. This book helps a person to understand the true value of life and live it to its fullest. The main objective of this book is to make each human being realize that nothing in this world is impossible. Even the word 'IMPOSSIBLE' says 'I M POSSIBLE'. All you need is to first make up your mind and look towards your task in a positive manner. You need to be self-confident to concentrate on your goal. Correct and organized planning is needed, there should be proper management of time, the right decisions have to be made, you need to stop giving excuses and many such topics are addressed.

We are living in the 21st century and life is moving at a very fast pace. To cope with this fast-moving life, we need to increase our speed too. It is necessary to leave behind the old trends and beliefs and look forward to life in a more practical manner.

The main part of the human body, which makes up a person's character, nature and behaviour, is his mind. The human mind has tremendous powers. A person might never have thought of the extent of the powers a human mind possesses. Most of the people are unaware of hypnotism, which is related to our day-to-day life. In order to lead a proper life, it is necessary for every human being, whether a child or an adult, to understand and acquire the knowledge of the mind and hypnotism. Such knowledge makes a person confident and his level of maturity and understanding also improves. A deep explanation of the mind and of hypnotism has been given very clearly in the book for everyone to understand in a very easy manner. The study of such topics changes one's way of thinking. Other than these topics, one should have clear ideas about the topics discussed below.

What is success? Different people have different definitions for success. Defining success for oneself is the first step towards achieving it. In this world, everyone wants to be successful, but what is the actual meaning of success? Success is a feeling of accomplishment. When we accomplish a certain task—professional or personal, we feel that we have been successful.

It is always said that, "An aimless life is a meaningless life." Learning the importance of a career and setting some goals in life is very necessary. Living a life without any goal is like walking on a road without any destination. Having a goal in life and knowing the manner by which we achieve it, helps us to understand the true value of life.

The main thing that brings about a change in one's personality and in his way of doing and presenting things is his confidence. Our confidence can help us to reach heights we have been unable to think of. It is an inner power and the one who realizes it, finds a way to convert his dreams into reality. There are many people who lack self-confidence in whatever they do. Lack of confidence can make the right things go wrong but self-confidence can make wrong things go right. This book is meant to help a person develop self-confidence and work with a positive attitude.

Whenever we take up a task, we must first accept ourselves as we are. Success can make you feel successful, only if you accept yourself. If you don't, then nothing will make a difference. Therefore, this book helps you to accept yourself as you are and enjoy each moment of your life.

There are many people who live under a certain kind of fear and this fear does not allow them to live their life with complete fulfilment. Fear resides in one's mind and nowhere else. One has just to look for the root cause of the fear and find a way to eliminate it. This book will help a person to overcome such fears.

Whatever we do, we need to do it with complete concentration. Only then can we do it in the best way. If our mind keeps revolving over different matters, we lose interest in the work that we are actually supposed to do. Concentration is the ability required to focus all our attention towards the one work that is undertaken. A person whose concentration level is high will also be good at problem solving and decision-making. Everyone, whether a child or an adult, wants to improve his level of concentration, but how to do it? Well, there are various exercises for it, but the best way to improve the power of concentration is MEDITATION. Meditation is the only way to attain peace and relax the mind and body in this competitive and commercial world. It helps us in many ways. Meditation has many benefits. The one who meditates remains cool, calm and fresh for a much longer time. Meditation helps a person to realize his real self and experience the super conscious mind. A complete step-by-step process of meditating has been given in this book. Many people say that they do not have the time to meditate. Well, we all know that time is the most precious commodity but only a few are able to understand the true value of time and use it in the most effective manner. People who say that they do not have time to do something are people who actually do not know how to do it or are not willing to do it. Each one of us has 24 hours per day. Not having time is just an excuse for not doing the work. We can do as much work as we want to; all we need is proper planning and the ability to manage time. Proper planning is necessary so that we can plan all our work, and time-management is necessary so that we can do all the work planned at the proper time. This book provides all the methods for better planning and time-management.

Another ability that is necessary in a person is decision-making. This ability makes a person independent and helps him to face the different challenges of life.

Decisions have their value only when they are made at a proper time. Decision-making helps a person at every step of his life. One wrong decision can lead him in a totally different direction. Whenever we make a decision, we first need to be in a relaxed state of mind, for when our mind is not relaxed, we can't think clearly. We also start behaving in a different manner. We need to keep our mind cool, calm and relaxed, only then we can do our work in the most effective manner. This book provides many methods for a person to remain in a relaxed state of mind.

No task can be achieved without hard work and determination. Success does not come by luck but is the result of a lot of hard work and practice. One has to work hard if one wills himself to achieve something. 'There is no gain without pain.'

There are people who feel that others must come and encourage them in whatever they do. One must understand that encouragement is an act of giving support, courage and hope. It is meant for those who are not self-confident and do not have sufficient self-assurance. Encou-ragement is not a necessity. If one is confident, determined and courageous, then encouragement from others does not make any difference. Once we start our work, then support and help come automatically.

We must keep doing our job without comparing ourselves with others. There may be some who might be better than you while some might not be. Comparisons are of no use. Along with comparisons, we must even stop competing with others. Trying to be better is a good habit but instead of being better than others, one must try to better oneself all the time.

This book helps a person to get complete knowledge of such matters that help a person to lead a proper life. It helps a person to realize his inner abilities and use them in the most effective manner. One who seriously goes through the entire book will definitely change his personality, his lifestyle and his way of thinking. He will become an open-minded person with a positive attitude and will also get rid of many of his bad habits. His mind will become cool and calm and his working efficiency will also increase.

Therefore, always remember,

"ALL YOU NEED... IS IN YOU"

Mind

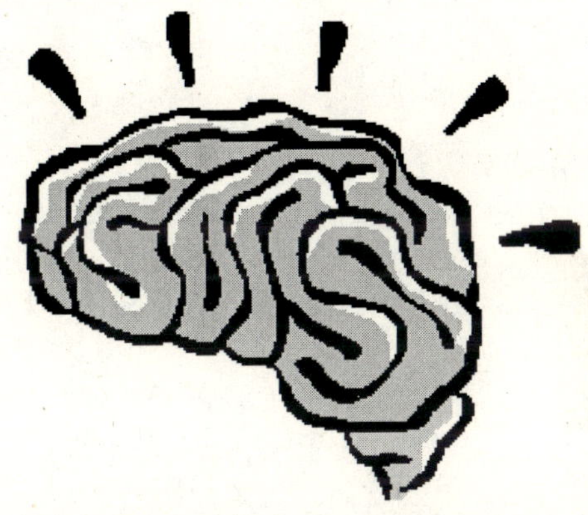

Mind is nothing but a small part of the human body. However, this small mind has the power to move the world, but only if one understands and uses it in a proper manner.

Many people created history and still there are successful people who are experts in their respective fields. There is no great difference between those successful persons and other common people. Every human body is made up of certain parts. Each normal human body has two legs, two hands, two eyes, ears, a nose, etc. Each human body has a heart and a mind. Each human body has a unique face.

Then what is it that makes every human being different from the other?

Yes, it is true that each one of us has a mind but each one uses it differently, which is what makes each individual different. Our mind has great powers stored in it. We can achieve anything that we wish to, only if we use our mind properly and effectively. Our mind has tremendous powers, the extent of which we have no idea. Nevertheless, if you seriously think, realize and understand its powers, it will definitely change your way of living and help you to proceed towards a better lifestyle. I am sure that the proceeding pages will help you in doing this.

The human mind has three stages:-

- ***Conscious Mind***

  It is a stage of mind in which a person is absolutely awake, active and alert; that aspect of the mind that thinks, reasons and discusses. One should always think from the conscious mind. Proper and correct decisions can be taken only by the conscious mind. People working from the conscious mind are adjustable and are comfortable to talk to. They are good listeners and perfect learners.

- ***Subconscious Mind***

  The subconscious mind is very useful and powerful if used in a proper manner and very dreadful if one does not understand it. The subconscious mind never thinks on its own but can be influenced by other people or even by the surrounding environment. Love, lust and attraction are all the result of the influence of someone or something on one's subconscious mind. It is a sort of storehouse of our memories. A person can never forget the things that are stored in his subconscious mind. A person who works from his subconscious mind feels that he is always right in whatever he does even if he is not. He is neither a good listener nor a good learner.

- ***Super Conscious Mind***

  Super conscious mind is the purest and the most miraculous part of the human body. It has such powers that a person can't even think of. It is a place with no bad thoughts and no impurities, a place filled with peace and generosity. When it is experienced, it is the most pleasant moment of life. It is always fresh and clean. It is our inner-self.

This was just a brief explanation about the three different stages of the mind.

Different people have different attitudes and different natures. Some of them are adjustable, open-minded, understand matters properly, accept changes with a positive attitude; they think over matters and discuss them when they find something wrong. Such people work with their conscious mind.

Talking about the subconscious mind, the most interesting thing about it is that for any person, his subconscious mind is always right. If it is stored in a person's subconscious mind that the person he is living with is good, humble and kind-hearted, then he will always treat him in a good manner and support him even if he finds that the person is doing wrong deeds. This is due to the influence of the person and the environment on his subconscious mind. Sometimes, you get attracted by a celebrity or start loving somebody. This is because that particular person has an influence on your subconscious mind and you begin to regard even his negative points in a positive light. This phenomenon of the subconscious mind of being influenced by somebody or something is known as HYPNOTISM, about which I have discussed later in the book.

Therefore, you can understand that all the emotions like love, hatred, jealously, anger, etc, proceed from the mind and not from elsewhere.

If there is a conversation regarding a certain topic, a person talking with his conscious mind will always treat it as a discussion while a person using his subconscious mind will consider it as an argument. This is because the person talking with his conscious mind understands that even his points regarding the topic can be wrong and so he discusses it. On the other hand, the person using his subconscious mind will try to insist that his point is right. He will never admit that he is wrong and so the conversation ends in an argument.

We often watch scenes of murder and robbery on television. We also watch the news telling us about terrorist attacks, bomb blasts, etc. Such news terrifies many people. People feel that humans who create such terror in society are no better than devils. Well, NO, they are not devils. They are very much like all others but their mind makes them different. They realize the power of their mind but instead of using it for their betterment, they use it for destruction and their mind is diverted towards the negative path. All this is due to the improper development of the mind. Right from childhood, they are shown the wrong path or they may have been affected by some incidents that might have left an impact on their subconscious mind. They feel that their subconscious mind is right and so they do whatever it says. Many a time, people do wrong deeds but do not realize that they are doing something wrong. These people are working with their subconscious mind.

If a particular image of a person is once stored in one's subconscious mind then one will always see him only in that manner. If your subconscious mind says that the person is bad, then you will never like to talk to him or see him even if he is good to you. In the same way, if the subconscious says that the person is right then you will always trust and believe him even if the person is deceiving you. You will never trust anybody who tries to expose him before you.

A profound explanation on the subconscious mind is given in the chapter titled HYPNOTISM.

The super conscious mind is the most miraculous stage of mind. It has the power to do anything. Experiencing it and having mastery over it is to have mastery over your entire body and once you master yourself then it is not very difficult to master others.

To get into the super conscious mind, one first needs to focus the conscious mind inwards and then clean up the impurities of the subconscious mind. When the conscious mind is directed outwards, it experiences the outer world and when it is directed inwards, it experiences the super conscious mind, which is our real self. The process of diverting our conscious mind inwards and deactivating the subconscious mind to go into the super conscious mind is known as MEDITATION.

STATES OF MIND

There are different states of the mind that we experience in our day-to-day life, but we are not aware of it. The most important thing about the mind is that it never stops. You may be doing any type of work like watching television, having your lunch, reading a book or anything else, all the time your mind keeps working. Even when you are doing nothing, just sitting comfortably and relaxing physically, your mind is moving around at different places.

Have you ever thought about what happens to your mind when you are asleep? When we are asleep, our body stops working; nevertheless, our mind keeps working. You might have noticed while travelling, we feel sleepy and close our eyes. We gradually go to sleep. However, when we hear some loud, unusual sound or when the car passes over a speed-breaker, we suddenly wake up. This is because even while we are asleep, our mind is working. We sometimes see some events or some unusual and disorderly images while we are asleep. We call them dreams. Well, dreams are generated from the subconscious mind. Sometimes, when we sleep, our conscious mind becomes inactive and we gradually slip into the subconscious mind. The subconscious mind becomes active and as it is the storehouse of all our memories, we see things that are revolving in the subconscious mind. These things can be senseless and meaningless. As your conscious mind was inactive while you were asleep, you don't remember what exactly you had seen in your dreams, when you wake up. Therefore, no matter what you are doing, your mind keeps on working 24 hours of the day.

Let us find out about the different states of the mind that we experience in our day-to-day routine.

NORMAL STATE OF MIND

This is the state in which your conscious mind is completely active and alert. One should always be in the normal state of mind. In this state, you are totally awake and the mind is directed towards the outer world. You are able to think, reason, question and react to different situations in a proper manner. You are totally in control of yourself.

SLEEPING STATE OF MIND

This is the state of your mind when you are asleep. Sleep can be of two kinds. One, when our conscious mind is active and the other, when it is not active.

Have you noticed dogs? When they sleep, they close their eyes, but on hearing some noise they suddenly wake up. This is because their conscious mind is active even when they are sleeping. This is not the case only with dogs but also with many other animals that have a mind. They include human beings as well. When we know that we do not have sufficient time to sleep or when we are asleep while travelling, our conscious mind is active. When we sleep at night, we want to be very relaxed. This is a sleep when our conscious mind becomes inactive. At midnight, when we are in deep sleep, we don't get up even if there is a loud sound or if somebody moves our body. We don't even register the touch of somebody. This is because at that moment, our conscious mind is not active. You will notice that in the mornings, we can hear all types of sounds and are aware of the happenings around us, even when we are sleeping on our bed. This is because in the morning, our conscious mind slowly begins to work.

DREAMING STATE OF MIND

In this state, the conscious mind becomes inactive and the subconscious mind is alert. This time, we go into a deep sleep and start dreaming. We have already discussed earlier about the area from where the dreams are generated. While we dream, our conscious mind is not active due to which, when we wake up, we do not remember what we had seen in our dreams. However, sometimes we are able to remember the dreams and even explain what we had seen in our dreams. These are the dreams we had seen in the mornings. We know that we have to wake up in the morning. Gradually as the sun rises, even our conscious mind slowly becomes active. Therefore, when our conscious mind is active, we will remember all that we had seen in our dreams.

HYPNOTISED STATE OF MIND

This is the state in which your mind and body is controlled by a person. The person can be yourself or somebody else. It could even be a hypnotist. A hypnotist can hypnotize you only by your wish and with your support. This is a state of mind in which a person takes complete control over your subconscious mind and gives suggestions or instructions to it. Your conscious mind can be either active or inactive. If you are hypnotized by a hypnotist then your conscious mind becomes inactive. Due to this, when you are brought back to the normal state you do not remember all that had happened with you. When you begin to love somebody or when somebody attracts you, you are in the hypnotized state of mind. In this state, you are more in control of your subconscious mind than of the conscious mind.

MEDITATION

Meditation is a process in which we have to concentrate deeply on our real self. This is the state of mind in which our conscious mind is directed inwards and the subconscious mind is deactivated. We gradually give up the contact with the outer physical world and enter the super conscious mind. This is the only state in which you can relax your body, especially your conscious and subconscious mind, and experience the super conscious mind.

Development of a Person and His Mind

Our birth and death are not in our hands; therefore, we can never change them. However, we can always improve the quality of our life. Life consists of various aspects; our childhood, teenage and so on. It is very necessary to understand these aspects of our life in order to live properly and effectively.

When a child is born, he is innocent. His mind is absolutely blank. His conscious and subconscious mind do not work. All he has is the super conscious mind, which is his real self. However, as the child grows up, gradually his subconscious mind starts working. Whatever parents or other elders put in his mind is stored there forever. God sends a child into the world as an individual. The child is unaware of who his parents and relatives are. The very first thing we teach a child is to recognize his parents and relatives. We tell him his religion; his name and give him his identity. All this is stored in the child's subconscious mind and so these things leave a permanent impression on his mind. Nobody can ever change these ideas easily. All this takes place within the first two years of his life.

The most crucial time in a child's life begins after it is two years old. During this time period, between the ages of two and nine, the child's mind works most powerfully. This is the time when a child develops his actual nature and behaviour. You'll find some people with an aggressive nature while some have a cool and charming nature; some have ego and pride while some have a humorous nature. They have developed this kind of nature according to what they had observed and how they were treated during their initial ages. After the age of two, a child listens, learns, observes and stores everything in his subconscious mind. This is the time when the foundation of a person's nature is laid through his observations and the things that are taught to him. A person's nature is totally dependent on the subconscious mind. He develops his nature and other things related to it on the basis of whatever is stored in his subconscious mind. That is why parents and teachers are advised to treat children in this age group with great care. This is the time when a child should be taught the values of life. If at this time, he is shown the wrong way, then it is very difficult to bring him back to the right path in the future. At this time, the child's conscious mind is not working, so he does not know what is right and what is wrong for him. He does not think on his own. He believes whatever he hears and watches, and develops himself accordingly. He observes his environment and everything that is happening around him. This is the time when a person's observation power works most effectively. From the age of seven onwards, gradually a child's conscious mind starts working. By the age of ten, a child's subconscious and conscious mind both start working. However, whatever is previously stored in the subconscious mind will always stay there.

As the child's conscious mind has now started working, he starts thinking on his own. He discusses matters that trouble him. He gradually develops the ability to take his own decisions. This is the period between the ages of ten and nineteen. This is the time when a person comes close to his friends. The influence of friends also affects the activities and development of the child; that is why it is said that you should keep good company. Since friends influence a child's mind, the company he keeps leaves an impression on him.

During this developing period, many physical changes take place and the child who enters his teenage years starts thinking that he is now a grown up. This is a period when a child needs proper guidance. He observes everything that is happening at home, the activities of his friends, the happenings in school and the things that take place as part of his daily routine. All these simultaneously affect his mind and his life. Nowadays, television, newspapers, magazines, etc. also play a big role in the development of the child's mind.

Now that the conscious mind has started working, the child ponders over all that he listens to and observes. He often gets confused and is not able to decide what is right and what is not. He also faces many problems due to sudden and unexpected happenings that take place in his life. At this point, a child tries to find a proper person who can help and guide him. Many children usually share their problems with their friends. They ask their friends for help, which is very dangerous; dangerous because at this point, clear and proper guidance is very necessary, which can never be got from friends who are in the same age group and who are facing similar problems and are themselves confused about various things. They are not experienced and mature enough to guide someone else, so, seeking help from friends should always be avoided.

Guidance and help should always be asked for from older people who are experienced, mature and who can understand the child's problems properly. The child could approach parents, teachers or any other elderly person. If at this time, a child does not get proper guidance, he commits mistakes. He might go on the wrong path or on the path that is not designed for him. This is a time when a child should concentrate on his career, start setting his goals, take up responsibilities and develop his own identity. In this period between the ages of ten and nineteen, a child should plan his career instead of wasting his time in unnecessary matters. If he starts thinking of his career at an early age, he will be able to begin his career early in life. In this age group, children, most of the time are confused and are not very serious regarding their career. They are not steady with their decisions. One day they will say that they want to study for an MBA degree, the next, they will say something else; meanwhile, if they see a 'cool' model, they get attracted and start thinking of modelling. Due to such folly, they waste their time during their teens instead of utilizing it to lead a better life.

However, if a child, in his initial years, is given proper knowledge about life, career and moral values, he would then move on the right path and attempt the right things. Nevertheless, a child's mentality changes during teenage. He starts living life on his own terms and so, wants to enjoy it to its fullest. But, a person should always REMEMBER, 'Anything extreme proves to be poisonous.' Therefore, enjoyment is fine as long as it is within limits. Life is meant to be enjoyed, but what is the meaning of enjoyment without a sense of dignity and self-respect? Extreme enjoyment has proved to be harmful as it is no longer enjoyment but craziness or madness. The earlier a teenager understands this phenomenon the better for him.

Hypnotism

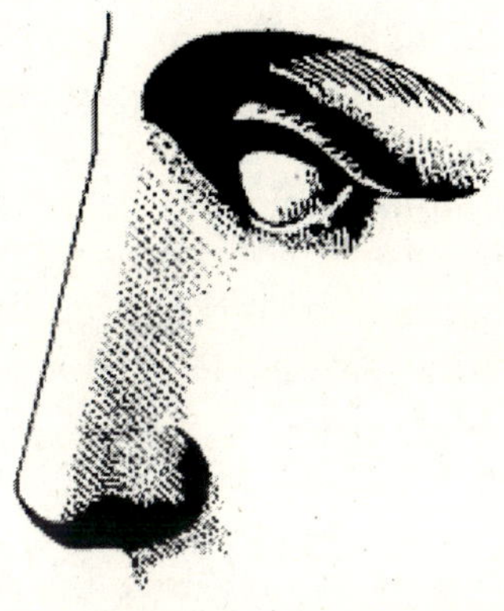

Hypnotism is a very vast subject. It is related to our day-to-day life. Very few people are aware of what the actual meaning and use of hypnotism is. Most of them think that it is related to tantra-mantra, or feel that it is nothing but an art aimed at fooling people. Some people associate hypnotism with magic. Different people have different definitions for it. Well, when the point comes to relating hypnotism with magic, we have to see that they are two different fields. Magic is just a trick; it is an art of presentation. Magic is totally based on science while hypnotism is a kind of science itself. Magic is not reality. If a magician makes things appear or disappear, it is just a trick to entertain the audience. But in hypnotism, if a hypnotist hypnotizes a person, then the person is actually hypnotized and does everything as ordered by the hypnotist. Magic involves the magician's confidence, concentration, will power and his way of presentation. When I am performing my magic shows, many people ask me whether I hypnotize my audience and show them only what I want them to see (*najarband*). Well, the answer is 'NO'. In magic shows people see everything that is happening in front of their eyes but since it is something difficult to believe, people consider it something more than just an illusion. However, hypnotism can never be related to magic.

Some are afraid of hypnotism while some find it interesting and exciting. Understanding the art of hypnotism is very necessary, as it is very beneficial.

Hypnotic techniques have been used since the ancient times but the practice of hypnotism has reduced because of its misuse or because of ignorance, misguided beliefs, and overstated claims. Many television clips and public performances of hypnotism have left a wrong impression of it in the minds of common people but today, again, this art is being revived. People are now curious to know about it. I know people who come to me to get knowledge about it and this has further encouraged me to write about it.

WHAT IS HYPNOTISM? HOW DOES IT WORK?

Hypnotism in totality is a science. The word hypnotism has been derived from the Latin word, hypnos, which means sleep. However, hypnosis is not totally related to sleep. It involves a more active and intense mental concentration. Hypnotized people can talk, write, and walk about. It can be termed as a state of semi-sleep. The phenomenon of making a person get into semi-sleep through different methods was then termed as hypnotism.

As explained in the first chapter of MIND, the human mind has three stages:

1) Conscious mind
2) Subconscious mind
3) Super conscious mind

Hypnotism is entirely related to the conscious and subconscious mind. When somebody or something, be it a person, thing or an incident, affects or influences your subconscious mind, you are hypnotized. However, the level of hypnotism may vary in accordance with the impact of the person, thing or incident on one's mind. If the impact is not very great, then the level of hypnosis is light. In such a state, the person's conscious mind may stay active but under the remit of the subconscious mind. If the impact is great, then deep hypnosis can be experienced. This can be experienced only when a person is hypnotized by a hypnotist or due to sudden unexpected shocks (death of dear ones, accidents, financial crises or any such bad news). In such a state, if a person is under a hypnotist's influence, complete anaesthesia (a state when a person is unable to feel anything) may be experienced and if it is due to other reasons then a person can go into coma or other states of unconsciousness.

Hypnotism is of three kinds:

- Being hypnotized by a hypnotist
- Being hypnotized by somebody or something unknowingly.
- Self-hypnotism

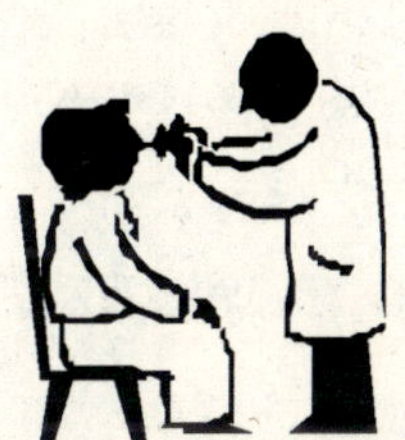

When you are being hypnotized by a hypnotist, you are giving the total control of your mind and body into his hands. The hypnotist has no special powers. The effects of hypnotism depend on the willingness and motivation of the person being hypnotized. No person can ever hypnotize you if you do not follow the simple steps or instructions that you are asked to. A hypnotist tries to gain your complete confidence and concentra-tion by your permission and support. Through his techniques, he deactivates your conscious mind and achieves total control over your subconscious mind. Because of this, you start doing all that the hypnotist commands your subconscious mind. However, when you are brought back to the normal state of mind, you don't remember anything that had happened to you, when you were hypnotized. This is because; the hypnotist had deactivated your conscious mind to enter the subconscious mind. Therefore, you were not aware of what was happening to you when you were hypnotized.

Sometimes we are hypnotized by somebody or something unknowingly. This is when something influences or leaves an impact on our subconscious mind and the conscious mind gets attracted towards that particular thing or matter. You might have noticed many children who know nothing about what they want to do in their life but when asked, will answer that they want to become a doctor, as their father is a doctor, or a teacher, as they love the teacher in their school, or a cricketer as they love watching cricket on television. This is because different things influence different people. A child who is not at all aware of what he is going to do for the next ten days can quite easily say what he wants to become after ten years, just because his mind has been influenced by that particular career. This is like being hypnotized unknowingly.

EXAMPLES OF BEING HYPNOTIZED UNKNOWINGLY:

When a boy and a girl love each other, they are even ready to die for each other. People say that their hearts can never be separated. REMEMBER, love and all other emotions like anger, jealousy, hatred, etc. are generated from the mind and not from the heart. The boy and the girl have been influenced by each other and are ruling over each other's conscious mind. Therefore, they will help and support each other even if one finds the other doing some wrong deeds. This is because their conscious mind is partially active. Their conscious mind is in control of the other person. If for any reason, there is a break-up between the two, they stop loving each other. Those two who were ready to die for each other, don't even like to see each other's face. This is because, the influence is over and they are back to their consciousness. Therefore, love is also a sort of hypnotism.

Often we watch advertisements on the television and get attracted by them. The advertisements are made in such a manner that they affect our mind and we happily buy the product. In the same way, when a salesman knocks at the door, at first we are often not willing to buy the product, but if the salesman is good and well experienced, then he creates such an influence on our mind that we get prepared to buy the product. This is also a sort of hypnotism, where advertisements and salesmen create an influence on our subconscious mind and get their work done.

Sometimes, we get attracted by a celebrity or create idols and have role models. We just watch a person on television, read about him in the newspapers and magazines and listen about him from friends and cousins and start liking him. We make such a person our role model. A person whom we have never met and talked to becomes an idol for us. We see him only on television and know nothing about his personal life, still we wish to become like him. This is because the personality and attitude of the celebrity affects our subconscious mind and the celebrity hypnotizes us unknowingly.

We find different people believing in different religions. Some believe in Christianity, some in Islam, some in Hinduism, Jainism or Buddhism. There are many religions and each religion has a huge number of followers. Every religion says and every human being knows that God is one. Some people go to the temple to pray, some to the church, while others go to the mosque or to other religious places. We know that God is one yet we have divided ourselves in the name of God. No religion states that the other religion is not good. All religions are based on their own concepts. If you ask a child, who he is, the answer will be that he is a Hindu, a Muslim, a Christian or from some other religion. This is because from the initial age, it has been stored in a child's mind that he belongs to one particular religion. He has been taught all the religious beliefs. He is taken to religious places and all this has an influence over his subconscious mind due to which he becomes a strong believer of a particular religion. A person also starts feeling that those people following a religion other than his are not good, and he starts having a different kind of feeling for them. Some people get so involved in their religion that they are ready to do anything for it. This is when a person's subconscious mind is extremely influenced by his particular religion.

Many gurus and saints are trying to popularize their respective religions. They influence people by religious speeches and deeds. This is also a state of hypnotism in which a person does not use his conscious mind and other people (saints or gurus) influence his subconscious mind. People become followers of such saints and begin to take greater interest in their religion. They even start believing in superstitions.

The main thing is to understand here is that you believe in a certain religion because your subconscious mind has been influenced by it. You have been hypnotized by it. If you think with your conscious mind, you will then realize and understand that we are all children of one Supreme God. We need to believe in that God and not the different religions, gurus or saints.

DIFFERENCE BETWEEN HYPNOTISM AND MESMERISM

When talking about hypnotism, many people connect the word mesmerism with it. Well, hypnotism and mesmerism are two different stages. When a person is hypnotised, his conscious mind is active while when he is mesmerized his conscious mind is deactivated. When you are mesmerized your body becomes like a machine, which works only on the orders and instructions that are given to it. In hypnotism, somebody or something influences your subconscious mind, but still your conscious mind is working. As there is no great difference between hypnotism (vashi-karan) and mesmerism (sammohan), people tend to relate them to each other.

In this way, you can understand how hypnotism is related to our day-to-day life but hypnotism is used in other areas too.

USES OF HYPNOTISM

Nowadays, the use of hypnotism has increased. Modern methods of hypnotism have helped scientists increase their understanding of the human mind and body. Hypnotism is used in research in the field of medicine and in psychotherapy. Hypnosis has occasionally been used in legal cases also.

A totally hypnotized person may experience changes in alertness, innovative thoughts and wakefulness. Physical changes within the body also may be produced if proper suggestions are put forward. They can include changes in the flow of blood, heart rate, blood pressure and sensations of cold and heat.

Therefore, doctors have been using it to treat certain illnesses. As the entire nervous system in a human body is controlled by the mind, hypnotizing the patient and giving select instructions to his subconscious mind can solve many physical problems.

Doctors use deep hypnosis as a form of anaesthesia, so that patients feel no pain while undergoing certain surgery or so that women do not suffer while they are giving birth to a child. Hypnotism has also been used to lessen the discomforts of patients recovering from surgery or other medical procedures.

When we are hurt or wounded, we feel pain. This pain is felt by the mind. If your mind insists that a particular part of the body is in pain then you feel the pain, but if the mind refuses to feel the pain, no pain will be felt. If a patient who is being operated upon is hypnotized and given proper instructions, he feels no pain.

Other than in purely physical treatment, hypnotism plays a major role in the work of psychiatrists and psychologists to help patients in problem solving or to treat patients suffering from mental problems like headaches, inferiority complex, anxiety, stress, imaginary fears, phobias and depression.

A person can get rid of his bad habits like smoking, drinking, etc. through hypnotism. If the person is hypnotized and is told about the evil effects of his bad habits or is given suggestions that he is capable of giving up all his bad habits, then these suggestions will be stored in his subconscious mind and he will give up the bad habits when he is brought back to the normal state.

When hypnotized, a person is in his subconscious mind and his conscious mind is not active. Whatever we do, act or see is stored in our subconscious mind. After a person has been hypnotized and is questioned regarding any matter he will speak only the truth because to speak a lie one needs to use one's conscious mind. Therefore, nowadays, hypnotism is also being used with witnesses and victims of crime. In hypnosis, people may remember important clues, such as a criminal's physical appearance or any other noteworthy detail that might help in solving the crime.

Until now you kept on reading about what hypnotism is and what happens if somebody hypnotizes you and in what areas hypnotism is used. Now, let us learn something about SELF-HYPNOTISM.

Hypnotism is all about controlling one's subconscious mind. If you control your own mind then it is known as SELF-HYPNOTISM. In self-hypnotism, you are in total control of yourself. You yourself give suggestions to your subconscious mind by keeping your conscious mind totally active. SELF-HYPNOTISM is very difficult but greatly beneficial.

If you have certain bad habits, you can get rid of them without the help of a doctor or a hypnotist. If you continuously keep reminding your subconscious mind about the evil effects of the bad habits and if you instruct the subconscious mind that you are capable of giving it up, you will then gradually move away from those habits. It is difficult but effective.

The only principle of SELF-HYPNOTISM is to continuously keep reminding your subconscious mind and keep instructing it about what you want to do and store it there so that it gradually begins working.

SELF-HYPNOTISM is helpful in many ways. It helps you to recognize your real self and improve yourself whenever and wherever necessary. It helps you to get rid of all your worries and tensions. It makes your mind cool and calm. You become an open-minded person and start working with your conscious mind. You give up your bad habits like smoking, drinking and others, if any. No person or thing is able to make an influence over the subconscious mind. You start understanding matters properly, your mind becomes more creative and the level of concentration increases. By SELF-HYPNOTISM, you will start understanding your mind and its power. As a result of this, your will power and the level of confidence will also increase. There are various other benefits of SELF-HYPNOTISM. It changes your entire personality. You will stop being rude and angry with others and move ahead in life with a positive attitude.

I, being a magician, have to perform my shows every evening with oomph and energy. Even though at times I am hurt or not well, I never wish my show to be cancelled. Be it a headache, stomach ache, sickness or injury, the show must go on. I have always been on the stage to entertain my audience. I have not had to bear pain; because I just did not feel it. Nevertheless, after the show is over, I am immediately taken to the hospital in case of acute physical problems but during the show my mind never accepts the pain, as it was of least importance to me. This is the power of self-hypnotism.

A complete knowledge about hypnotism and SELF-HYPNOTISM leads a person towards living a better life. When this knowledge is clear in a person's mind, he can work more confidently and effectively. Hypnotism can help a person in any field and at any place. With its help, his power of convincing increases. His personality along with his conversation becomes so impressive that it influences other people. Therefore, having complete knowledge of hypnotism leads a person towards living a successful life.

Success

WHAT IS SUCCESS?

Success in today's life cannot be measured in terms of school, college or technical education alone. We need a lot of practical knowledge and various skills to overcome day-to-day challenges in life, whether they are professional or personal.

To some people success means possessing materialistic objects such as bungalows, cars, and much more and they make it their main objective in life. For such people, acquiring maximum wealth means being successful.

For some people, the definition of success is to be self-satisfied and happy in whatever they do, even if they do nothing. They feel successful in living a life of complete fulfillment. For them success is enjoying whatever they do.

Some people define success as the achievement of set goals in life. For such people, success is a ladder on which they take one step upward at a time and gradually proceed towards the goal. Setting a goal, achieving it and then planning again for new goals; this is what they define as real success.

Some people have a personal mission in life. For such people fulfilling their personal mission is achieving success.

The definition of success may be different for different people. How to define success for oneself is very important. If you don't have a clear definition of success for yourself then you can never achieve it because if you don't have a perfect explanation for what you want to achieve then you are not able to prepare your path to reach it. The first step to achieve success is to define it for yourself. If you do not have a personal definition of success you are unsuccessful and you gradually become frustrated with your career and life. Until you understand the meaning of success, it is impossible for you to be successful.

However, your definition of success should be such that while you achieve your well-planned task you are emotionally happy and physically healthy. If you achieve your goal but you are not happy with the achievement, then the success is of no use as there is no self-satisfaction. Even if you achieve your goal and you are happy about it but are not able to enjoy and cherish it because you are not physically fit, then the success cannot be termed as complete. Success means being able to achieve your goal while you are physically fit and with a feeling of self-satisfaction.

A person needs three keys to open the doors to success and those three keys are:

- Concentration

- Confidence
- Hard work

Concentration in your work
Confidence within yourself
Hard work to achieve your goal

If you have these three keys with you then no power on the earth can keep you away from opening the doors to success.

FAILURES LEAD TO SUCCESS

Success lies at the tip of the mountain of effort and hard work. However, scaling this mountain is quite difficult. You may meet many obstacles on your way but if you stop then there is no other way to reach to it.

You may be disappointed if you fail but you will be doomed if you don't try.

—Beverly Sills

Our failures are the biggest reasons for our unhappiness. Nobody likes failures. Therefore, as failures are never intentional, we should always try to find the reason for our failures, understand it and learn from it. Instead of considering it as our disability or bad fortune, we should take it as an opportunity to start something again with better knowledge and experience. Our failures give us a chance to improve ourselves. Always REMEMBER, disadvantages are simple roadblocks that we need to cross on our journey towards success.

You may fail many times but you aren't a failure as long as you keep trying. If you fail once and don't try again and accept the failure then you can never achieve success. Stopping and declaring yourself a failure proves that you have no confidence and don't want to improve. Failures should be accepted with strength and courage, only then these failures will lead you to success.

Failure doesn't mean that you have lost the game; it is just another opportunity for you to start all over again with a little more wisdom. When you fail once then in the next attempt you try harder and you are sure to succeed because you know the reason for your failure and you are definitely not going to repeat the mistake. All you need is to persevere and not discourage yourself by accepting yourself as a failure.

Most successes are built on failures.

—Charles Chow

Failure is the result of lack of understanding of the mission or lack of hard work. You are allowed to take up whatever task you wish to but it is important for you to first know your target clearly, prepare and understand the plan to reach it and work towards it with complete heart and mind.

REMEMBER,

Failure is the tide when persistence is at its ebb.

There is the greatest practical benefit in making a few failures early in life.

—Thomas H. Huxley

Therefore, never run away from failure. When you fail, think about the reason for your failure and make another attempt, but do not repeat the mistake, keep on going and you will find that success is not too far.

Once you are successful in your task, don't feel that it

is the end. Actually, it is just the beginning.

Once when a journalist was interviewing me, he asked me a very rarely asked question, "At what height do you find yourself? What part of success do you think you have achieved?" I found it a very interesting question. I replied, "If you ask me at what height I find myself, my answer will be that I am just at the door that leads to success." I added, "If you ask me the same question after ten years, my answer will be the same. If questioned after twenty years, I'll answer that I am still at the starting point because for me success has no end. I don't feel that a person can ever stand still and say that he has achieved success in totality. Success is never-ending. It is an ongoing process. I cannot ever say that I have achieved a certain part of success as I believe that success can never be measured."

Never feel that you have achieved everything. Our life is too short and the list of achievements is never-ending. Dreams, desires, wishes, achievements are some things that have no end. Even if you have achieved a lot, still at the last moment of your life, you will find that there are many things yet to be achieved and many tasks yet to be fulfilled. Therefore, one should always REMEMBER that success has no end.

Goal

Goals lead to a purpose in life. It is the starting point of success. Aim at the moon. If you miss it, at least you will hit one of the stars. Our life becomes meaningful only when we have a goal in life. As I said earlier, living life without any aim is like walking on a road without any destination.

If we can sleep and dream at night, we can make those same dreams come true but only if we want to and have the ability to make them come true.

If we do not have a goal in life, our life becomes meaningless and we are not able to understand the true value of our life. A goal gives us a genuine reason to live.

The process of setting goals helps one to choose where he wants to go in life. If you know precisely what you want to achieve, you are then able to direct your efforts towards the right place. You are also able to quickly identify the distractions that would otherwise lure you from your track.

Ask any human being about what he wants to do in future and the most common answer you'll get is that he wants to lead a comfortable and happy life. He wants to achieve something or accept life as it comes to him.

There are two ways to live a life.

1. Accept life as it comes.
2. Lead life as we want to.

In the first case, we accept life as it comes. Our life is not planned. We are waiting to discover what the future holds for us. It could be sorrows or happiness... life could be thrilling, terrifying or exciting. We do not know. People want to be happy and so they keep adjusting to the various situations in their lives. They have big dreams and desires but want to lead a happy and comfortable life instead of setting and planning some goals and fulfilling their desires. They wait for each new day to see what it will unfold for them. ***Accepting life as it comes*** is merely adjusting ourselves to situations. We get to live our life once and so instead of adjusting to it, it's better to lead it as we want to.

In the second case, we plan our life. We live as we want to. We do not wait for our future. On the contrary, we make our future in our own way. We prepare some short-term and long-term goals, plan for them and work towards achieving them. We work with complete determination, concentration and confidence. When we achieve them, we feel a certain type of happiness: a happiness of accomplishment, a happiness of fulfilment, a happiness that cannot be explained but only realized.

The person who selects the first way of living is like a traveller on an unknown road who does not know where he really wants to go or where the road is going to take him. He is just travelling and preparing himself for the next happening; it could be either a rough and harsh road or a smooth one. There could be a stream ahead or a speed-breaker, you never know.

On the other hand, a person who leads a life as he wants to is like a traveller who is travelling on a road that is made by him. He is aware of where he wants to go and where the road is leading. He prepares his road himself. Now, you have to decide, what sort of traveller are you?

If you want to make your own living and live life to its fullest, you need to make some changes and adjustments in life. If you want to achieve something different, then you need to do something different. If you keep doing all that you had always been doing, then you will get all that you always had. Whatever you want to achieve or become is entirely a matter of your choice, but to be successful in your task you first need to clearly define and understand what your task actually is. Instead of just sitting and thinking about the goal, you need to put your plans into actions in order to achieve the goal.

So dear readers, it is never too late. Just decide your goal and start your journey towards success. You should be very clear about what you want to achieve. Big talks and desires are useless. Your goals should be specific and must have some base. They should be realistic and believable. If you don't believe that you can achieve your goal, then you will never be able to achieve it.

Firstly, ensure that the goals that you want to achieve are made by your personal choice and interest. Being advised by elderly persons is always good. However, no choice is worth it if it is made under pressure. Your goals should be what you want to achieve and not what your parents, spouse, family, or employers want them to be.

Begin by writing down your goal, for a goal that is not written is not a goal but just a desire or a wish. When it is written down, it becomes a commitment. A commitment that you shall always remember. It keeps reminding you that there is still a task that is not yet accomplished. A commitment is something that helps you keep going even after your enthusiasm and motivation is lost. A goal becomes just a thought of the mind when it is not written down, a thought that can be forgotten easily or changed.

Ninety-seven per cent of the human beings do not reach their goals because they do not write them down.

Therefore, decide your goal, write it down on a paper and paste it on your study table or write it in a book. Read your goals regularly so that they keep reminding you about your tasks. This brings you back to the right track if you forget or lose your path.

The path that you may select to achieve your goal may not always be as easy as you expect it to be, but always remember, *everything is difficult, before it is easy.* The fire of progress must keep burning in you and the flame must be so bright that no obstacle can extinguish it.

You will always meet with twists and turns on your way towards your goal. There will always be an impression of difficulties; you will come to crossroads when you are confused. Your relationships may act as speed-breakers and try to make your path more difficult. There will be a downslide of many disappointments and dissatisfactions and on the other hand, you might have a steep climb with loads of responsibilities. Your family will be the check-post where you will have to halt, but however tough the path may be, you can easily go along it when you drive the car of confidence with the tyres of hard work and the engine of hope and desire. If you drive this car with full concentration and proper planning, you can traverse any path however rough or tough it may be. One should not give up because a thing is difficult, on the contrary, the more difficult a thing is, the more determined one should be in his attempt to succeed.

You should have one main goal in life: a clear goal that defines your career, your future. Along with this one main goal, there should be different short- term and long-term goals too, so that there is excitement and curiosity to do different things in life. You should set goals that could help you build your personality and your character. When you have different goals, life is full of excitement. These goals change our lifestyle. Rather than wasting our time in unnecessary matters, we involve ourselves in doing some useful and fruitful things. Short-term goals keep us on track and these are not very difficult. However, one thing should always be taken care of that no short-term goals should be in contrast to your main aim in life. All goals should relate to the one main goal. Only then, these goals are sensible and are of some use.

When you achieve such short-term goals, you experience a feeling of accomplishment. You feel far more confident than before. What you get when you achieve your goal is of much less importance than what you become in the process, which makes you feel good and happy. These accomplishments help you to move ahead on your path with more efficiency. Due to it, the speed at which you progress, increases. You feel that you are getting closer to your main goal. When you stand on the ground and look at the tenth floor of a building, it seems to be at a great height but when you climb up the stairs with firm determination, you find yourself progressing at every step. After having climbed each floor you feel happy because you are getting closer to your destination. As you find yourself getting closer to the destination, you keep going even if you feel tired. Therefore, these short-term goals are just like the steps of the building, the few long-term goals are like the floors and your main goal is the tenth floor, which is your destination.

Always think higher, higher and still higher. Never feel satisfied with what you have accomplished. You still have many more missions in life. Therefore, always do what you feel is right even if it is the most difficult thing to do.

Progress comes to an end if you stand still and think of what you have done or achieved in the past. Do not think of the past. It may be good or bad but whatever it is, it is over. Think of the present. Do not look behind, for it is gone. Always look ahead. Look at what you want to achieve and you are sure to progress. Do not move back, for a hero fears nothing, complains of nothing and never gives up. If he did, he would not be a hero.

There is a huge gap between what you are and what you can be. Ninety-five per cent of people read history but only five per cent create history. It is now entirely your choice to select your category. Do you include yourself in that ninety-five per cent or in that five per cent?

Forward, forever forward, at the end of the tunnel
is the light...
At the end of the fight, is the victory!!!

Confidence

Confidence is a feeling that you can trust and believe in. It is a belief in your own ability to do things and present yourself in the most attractive and effective manner.

Confidence is like the shoes with spikes with which you can win the race of life. Confidence can help one to reach unimaginable heights. However, we never try to realize this power in ourself and because of it we perform well below our capabilities. Lack of confidence can affect one on various occasions such as public speeches, interviews, examinations, etc. This is because where there is no confidence, there is a fear of being rejected or fear of failure. The fear inside us is going to take us nowhere. Confidence is what helps us to put our thoughts into words in a much better and more effective manner. Therefore, we should stay away from the kinds of fear that stop us from presenting ourselves before the world. Instead of being discouraged by these unending moments of fear, it is better if we work on ourself with the skills we have and with loads of confidence. Working with confidence will definitely help in our journey to success.

HOW TO BE CONFIDENT IN LIFE?

☞ Confidence is contrasted with fear. Where there is confidence there is no fear and vice-versa. Hence, it is always better to live with confidence than with fear. Fear resides in our mind and nowhere else. If there is any fear in our mind: fear of failure, rejection or any other, we shall not be able to keep our mind calm and will perform below our capabilities. Such fears prove to be drawbacks and cause a lack of confidence in a person and in everything he does in life. Therefore, the first step towards being confident in life is overcoming all our fears by putting them out of our mind. Fear raises many negative thoughts in our mind. Turning those negative thoughts into positive ones may help you to get rid of them. Try to change your way of thinking and reacting to situations and replace the negative questions arising in your mind with positive and encouraging thoughts.

Negative Questions	**Replace with**
"Will I be able to do it?"	"I should try it. It shall be a new experience."
"What if I fail?"	"I'll be progressing and even if I fail, I shall be aware of what is lacking in me."
"Will I be able to speak properly?"	"I shall prepare myself thoroughly and speak with complete wisdom."
"I failed the last time. What if I do not succeed again?"	"I got another chance. This time I shall make no mistakes and work with complete concentration."

It is how you feel, think and speak that changes your way of doing things. So feel good, fearless and positive and you shall be a confident person.

☞ Many people in this world are dissatisfied with various things in their life. It could be their tone of speaking, physical appearance, habits, work or even their family. If you are not happy and contented with yourself, it indicates that you have no confidence and if you are not confident about yourself, you cannot expect others to have confidence in you.

Your confidence will automatically be boosted if you accept yourself as you are. Only after you accept yourself can you display yourself and your abilities to the world in the best way possible. Every individual has certain good and bad aspects. REMEMBER, the negative aspects are for accepting and understanding (they can always be worked upon) while the positive ones are for realizing and developing. Instead of thinking about your weaknesses, you should concentrate on your strengths. By doing this, you are reminding yourself that you too possess some unique qualities. Your aim should be to improve yourself; hence, you should focus on yourself and your skills instead of watching others and comparing yourself with them. Instead of searching for another person's good quality in yourself, try to realize, develop and respect your own good qualities that might be lacking in others. This will help you to develop a feeling of confidence.

☞ One must try to understand the value of positive thinking. At the office, the boss assigned an employee the responsibility of managing a complete presentation. This was his first presentation and he was not confident. The first thoughts that struck him were, "Will I be able to do it? What if I make a mess of it?" he thought that he might fail and so he did not accept the task. The boss handed it over to some other person and the work was done properly. However, if the employee had been a confident person, he would have gladly taken up the task and would have worked hard for his first presentation to be a success. Having knowledge and knowing all the facts and figures is not enough. You should also have the confidence to expose your knowledge and skills on appropriate occasions, otherwise it may keep one away from many good opportunities in life and to reach the position you deserve.

Therefore, in order to get rid of such negative thoughts, all you need is to think positive and try to do things without any hesitation. You should keep reminding yourself that when you make an attempt, you might succeed or you might fail, but inaction is absolute failure. So, why not attempt with confidence. Do every work with an open heart and mind and with the hope of success. If you want to do something and if you know how it has to be done than just prepare your mind for it and go for it without thinking of anything else. If you succeed your confidence will automatically increase and if you don't, you shall at least realise what is lacking in you. You shall get the experience of attempting something, which will surely be useful in the future. Whenever you have a problem while at work, say to yourself, "I can do it and I will do it." Whenever you are blocked by a difficulty, say to yourself, "I will overcome it." By having such positive and challenging thoughts in mind, you are motivating yourself and due to this, you will find your confidence growing.

☞ If you always keep thinking over your mistakes and failures of the past, you will get nowhere. What is done, is done and you cannot change it. It is no use thinking upon the matter and wasting time by being disappointed about the past. You should concentrate on your present and on what has to be done. If you keep your mistakes and failures on your mind and always feel guilty for them than you shall never be able to accept yourself and if you do not accept yourself than even others will not. Keeping such thoughts in mind stops you from progressing and decreases your efficiency. Mistakes and failures are for learning. They are not purposeful or intentional. Therefore, one should consider them as a learning experience and move ahead in life with wisdom and understanding.

"Believe in yourself. Soon, others will believe in you too."

☞ Attitude is a very important word in the dictionary of success. It is the way you think and feel about somebody or something. Having read the points given above, you must have understood that to be confident, you first need to have a positive attitude. Whether it is a teacher, doctor, parent, salesperson, student or an employee, nobody can be good in his or her job without a positive attitude. A person with a positive attitude will always say 'YES' to whatever work is given to him if he knows how to do it. Therefore, try to have a positive attitude towards yourself and everything you do in your life. This will definitely make you a confident person.

It is very important to be confident in life but remember; you should try to increase your confidence to the level that is necessary or else it may lead to over-confidence, which proves to be very harmful. Over-confidence results in dissatisfaction or it may make a person egoistic; a person then starts talking big just to maintain his ego. Ego and pride are the results of over-confidence. One should be confident enough to earn appreciation. Over-confident people are ignored. They gradually become lonely and frustrated.

"Confidence is all about being cool, calm and relaxed."

Therefore, always REMEMBER, you yourself are your greatest helper. Nobody else can help you to gain confidence. Realize your inner power and try to convert your dreams into reality.

"For they conquer who have confidence and believe they can."

Accepting Yourself

"I can't do it."
"I don't have the ability to do this work."
"I am not as attractive as the other person."
"I am not confident enough to complete this task."
"I am not well experienced for this work."

This negative attitude can never bring success in life. If you don't feel good about yourself, even others won't. REMEMBER, success is all about liking yourself and whatever you do. Each one of us is a unique person with a different appearance and different abilities. If you feel that you don't have the qualities that others have, than you should take a look at yourself and be proud of the qualities that you have and which are lacking in others. Instead of feeling discouraged about what you do not have, you should realize and take advantage of what you have. Various people in this world are unhappy and discouraged by one thing or the other. Some are not satisfied with their appearance, while some do not like their tone of voice. Some are not happy with their environment or family while some are discouraged due to some incident or accident that occurred in their life. Different people have different problems, which they are not ready to face. What do you think about such people?

We are what God has made us and we need to accept that not all things are in our hands. We might wish to change many things but we cannot and this fact should never be denied. Things that cannot be changed should be accepted with courage. Life is not a glass of milk into which we can add the flavour of our choice. We should look towards every unfortunate situation in life with a positive attitude and move forward. Brooding on the matter destroys a person's equinamity and the result is frustration or depression. Whatever you are and whatever you have, you need to accept it. If you want to progress towards a better living, you first need to accept where you are, only then you can reach where you want to.

People forget that nobody in this world is perfect. Instead of concentrating on the good things, they give great importance to the one thing that is not perfect and keep dwelling on it. Therefore, accept yourself as you are and face the challenges of life confidently without being disappointed about what life has not given you. On the contrary, be grateful to God for the kind of person you are, for you are a unique individual in this whole world. There is no second person like you. You can't be compared to anybody.

Hence, always be happy and satisfied with what you are and what you have. Stay as you are. To be successful, you do not need to copy successful people. Different people have different talents and go through different circumstances. Therefore, never try to imitate another's mode of life, which is not your own. Every human being has some specific hidden qualities. So do you. Find out and try to develop all those hidden qualities. Be yourself. You will feel uncomfortable and miserable when you try to become somebody other than the person in your own body. Don't pretend to be what you are not.

"By imitating a lion, nobody can become a lion."

Nobody has ever been exactly like you and nobody will ever be exactly like you. You were, you are and you will always be one and only one in this big, huge world. So, accept yourself with great confidence.

Envy is ignorance and imitation is suicide,
Whatever you are, accept yourself with pride.

Nevertheless, in future you can be whatever you want to be. You need to accept yourself as you are and keep improving yourself whenever possible. You need to work with confidence and with an inner spirit of achieving something.

Fear

Fear is one of the deadliest enemies of humanity. However, the most surprising thing is that man out of his own questioning mind creates this fear. It does not come from anywhere outside. It has no existence of its own. It is only a creation of one's wild and uncontrolled imagination. One's mind is the only residence of fear. Therefore, to get rid of fear, remove it from your mind and you'll find it nowhere in your life.

Fear is the most common negative emotion felt by humankind. These do not allow a person to relish and enjoy life. They become obstacles in the smooth running of our life even when you have everything in your favour.

It is very necessary for us to overcome our fears because they do not allow us to live our lives with complete fulfilment. Just preaching or listening to sermons from some sacred books will not conquer the fears of life. You need to understand the root cause of the fear and then search for some solution.

Nothing in life should be feared,
It is only to be understood.

If you notice, a fellow is always with you. He is with you day and night. He eats, drinks, walks, breathes and sleeps with you. He follows you wherever you go. Probably, he may be sitting beside you even at this moment while you are reading this book. In the evening, when you relax in a pleasant park for a while, you forget this fellow for some time, but suddenly you remember him and find him beside you. This fellow is none other then the fear in your mind. Through this I want to explain that fear is with you as long as you make a conscious effort to be aware of it. Once you relax yourself and divert your mind towards other things, it automatically disappears.

Sometimes, instead of the fear following you, you start following fear. This fear takes control of your mind and enjoys full power over you. This is because you have given it a lot of importance in your life. You have given it so much power that it has now become your master.

Fear is our greatest enemy. It is a thief who robs you of your joy, happiness, contentment and peace. Living a life with fear is a miserable life. You must conquer your fears if you wish to enjoy your life to its fullest.

A philosopher said, *"The basic cause of human misery is non-attainment of things we desire and fear of losing what we have achieved."*

Many a time, a person has a fear of losing something he has or has achieved.

- Fear of losing a job
- Fear of losing near and dear ones
- Fear of losing money, status or fame
- Fear of losing some precious things

We must try to get out of the mess of such fears that engulf us by identifying them through careful examination of our thoughts, feelings and find reasons and causes of our fears.

There could be many other fears like:

- Fear of being robbed
- Fear of failure in an examination
- Fear of being insulted
- Fear of public speaking
- Fear of being attacked by dreadful diseases
- Fear of separation from somebody or something
- Fear of an accident
- Fear of being rejected in an interview
- Fear of heights and darkness
- Fear of singing and acting on stage
- Fear of being punished
- Fear of death

The list could be as long as you and I wish. However, these fears can be conquered. All these fears exist only in the mind. You need to uproot the fear in your mind and thus stop its growth. Therefore, to control fear, you actually need to control your mind and imagination. Fears are nothing but thoughts and they always reside in a weak and questioning mind. They won't dare to stand against a strong and firm mind. So now, it depends upon you. Do you want fear to reside in your mind?

Robert Jones Burdette said, "There are two days in the week about which and on which I never worry. Two carefree days kept sacredly free from tension and apprehension. One of these days is YESTERDAY and the other day I do not worry about is TOMORROW".

If there is fear in you, it should be the fear of doing something evil. So let us rise every morning and make the following resolve for the day:

I shall not fear anyone on earth.
I shall only fear God.
I shall not bear ill will towards anyone.
I shall not submit to injustice towards anyone.
I shall conquer untruth by truth
And in resisting untruth

I shall put up with all my suffering.
I shall use my fear to help me to focus on my strength.
I shall defeat fear by believing in myself.

Concentration

"The ability to focus"

On a hot sunny day, the most powerful magnifying glass will not burn the paper if you keep moving the glass. Nevertheless, if you focus at one point, the paper has to burn. This is the power of concentration.

The ability to direct all your effort and attention on one thing at a time without thinking of anything else is your power to concentrate.

Whenever we start a new piece of work, the first thing needed for the work to keep going in a proper manner is our attention and concentration on that work. If we do our work with our mind somewhere else, then we cannot complete the work properly. Any work is completely and properly finished only when it is done with full concentration and determination. It is said that we should do only one piece of work at a time and while doing it we should think exclusively about it without diverting our mind towards anything else. This is because when we try to do two things at the same time, our attention and concentration is divided and neither is completed properly.

The difference between a good student and a weak student is determined by his power of concentration. In the class where all students are taught the same thing, why is it that only a few of them are able to perform well during their examinations? The reply is their inability to focus on their subject. Studying hard, learning the chapters and then forgetting. This situation commonly occurs with most of the students. This is the result of not studying with full concentration. While studying, their attention and concentration is sometimes diverted to other things like the programmes being shown on the television, friends playing outside, phone calls, the food being cooked in the kitchen or anything else. Due to lack of concentration, they forget whatever they had learned and their time is wasted.

A small child of three or four years is able to memorize the latest film songs with great ease and happiness but the same child finds it boring and extremely difficult, when asked to memorize the schoolwork. This is because the child is not interested in learning his lessons. When you do not have interest in something, you are not able to concentrate on it. Remember, to concentrate on something you first need to create your interest in that work. Only then you can enjoy doing your work.

A forty-eight year old gentleman said his prayers every morning at seven. Often he noticed that as he stood in front of God and tried to visualize His image in his mind, many unrelated thoughts such as the past happenings, things to be done during the day, office meetings, etc. came on the screen of his mind. He tried his level best not to think about them, but they kept coming back repeatedly. This was his daily problem. However, he never gave up. Every morning he prayed and tried not to think about anything that could distract him. Later on, his problem was totally solved.

This story tells us that there may be many obstacles on your way to success, but you should concentrate only on your goal. Unless you concentrate on your goal, you cannot achieve it. It can be difficult for you to concentrate, but it is a skill that can always be practiced.

The best way to improve your power of concentration is through meditation.

MEDITATION

All the external parts of the body are relaxed when we sleep or take rest but for the relaxation of the mind and heart one needs to meditate. Only through meditation, we can achieve complete peace of mind. It helps us to awaken our inner powers. During meditation, one enters into a unique state of mind, which is very beneficial for the body. It also helps the nervous system to work in a normal way.

Now, the question may arise in your mind that though meditation has many benefits, how can it help us to improve our power of concentration.

In meditation, the rays of the mind are focused at a fixed point. It is difficult to concentrate in such a way but as one keeps practicing, it becomes easy. As I said earlier, everything is difficult, in the beginning. If you keep meditating regularly, you yourself will find a change in you. Slowly, due to this practice, your power of concentration will improve. The complete step-by-step method of meditating has been given in the chapter titled MEDITATION.

This is the power of meditation, which helps you to improve your power of concentration.

There is a Latin proverb, "*If you run after two hares,*

you will catch neither."

Whatever work one has to do; the most vital requirement is to do it with complete concentration. Usually while working on one thing, we start thinking about something else. It could either be about a personal matter, about a conversation one recently had or about some recent happenings. While working on one thing, our mind gets diverted to many other things. REMEMBER, we have one mind that can do everything but should be used for only one job at a time. We should avoid diverting our mind from the main job towards other topics. I know that it is not as easy to do as it is to write about it, but there are techniques to get rid of such problems.

Here are a few of them: -

- Take a novel, storybook, magazine or a newspaper. Sit down quietly and let the music system play on. Let it play some of your favourite songs. Now, you have to read the book without diverting your mind towards the song being played. Concentrate on the reading material and try not to listen to the music. You not only have to read but even understand what you are reading. Let the music not divert your mind from the material you are reading. Your complete attention should be on the book and your ears should be deaf to the music.
- Place a table clock on your television set. Switch on the television to a music channel and let the volume be a bit loud. Sit a few steps away from the television set. Now, try to concentrate on the clock. Observe the seconds ticking by. Keep all your attention on it as it keeps ticking on. Let your mind not be diverted to the music or the video being played on the television below.

Initially, it will be difficult for you but as you keep practicing it will gradually start getting better. You can start by practicing for 2 minutes each day and keep increasing the time as per your wish and control. The basic idea is to focus on only one thing at a time, leaving everything else aside. The more you practice; the more will your level of concentration go up.

You can perform any activity you wish, but it should not have so much control over you that it can divert your concentration away from your goal.

Meditation

In this hectic, commercial and competitive modern life, people often feel stressed and over-worked. It seems like there is just not enough time in the day to get everything done. People are so busy that they feel that there is no time to stop and meditate. But, REMEMBER, by meditation you can occupy your day's time in a more effective way as it makes your mind calmer and more focused.

Meditation in the real sense is the key to control our mind. In meditation, you forget about all the worldly matters and get deep inside yourself. It is a process of concentrating completely on one particular object. During this process, you have your total attention on the object and you are not at all bothered about the outer world. You are aware only of yourself. This process quietens and calms the mind and makes it fresh for new thoughts and ideas. In this state of mind, you can derive as much peace and harmony as you wish to. The nervous system of a human body is controlled by its mind and as meditation relaxes and freshens the mind it also improves the working of the nervous system in our body and it helps us to remain cool, calm and fresh for a much longer time. This is the only way to relax our mind as well as our body in this competitive and commercial world.

HOW TO MEDITATE?

- One should meditate in the mornings as it is the most pleasant time and so that the day starts with fresh thoughts and ideas.
- The place should be quiet and clean. Quiet, so that it helps in concentrating and clean for better hygiene.
- It is best if you can meditate in an open and airy place, for fresh air pleases and freshens the mind.
- See to it that nobody disturbs you while you meditate.
- You need to sit comfortably in a traditional cross-legged posture with your back straight. This prevents your mind from becoming sluggish or sleepy.
- Meditation should be started by a breathing exercise. You must take in deep breath, hold it for few seconds and exhale. The process should be as slow as possible. Keep repeating for some time. This exercise makes your mind cool, calm and relaxed. It helps you to forget about all personal and professional matters.
- Along with the breathing exercise, you now need to slowly start concentrating on one particular thing or object. You should close your eyes and visualize an image on the screen of your mind. It could be a beautiful flower, a candle, a bird, a leaf, or a portrait. It could be anything as per your wish. All your attention and concentration must be on that particular object. Don't let anything distract your mind.
- There may be many other matters that might rise in

your mind. You need to avoid them and try concentrating on the image. If you find that your mind has wandered to other thoughts, immediately get back on track and concentrate.

- You can concentrate for as long as you wish and can. Then slowly open your eyes, rub your hands against each other and pass them over your eyes and face. The hands should touch the eyes and the face.
- Then slowly open your eyes and you are now ready to face the fresh day with a well-prepared mind and a relaxed body.

You must have seen many saints or other religious people meditating. Their way of meditating is different. These people take a position at a particular place and meditate. They meditate so deeply that they forget about the outer world. They are not aware of whatever is happening around them. They don't get disturbed or distracted by anything happening in their surroundings. They aren't aware even if you call them or touch them. This is because they direct their conscious mind inwards and so it leaves the contact with the outer world. They concentrate on their inner self, which is actually the super conscious mind. To experience the super conscious mind we first need to direct our conscious mind inwards and silent our subconscious mind. When the conscious mind is directed outwards, we experience the outer world and when it is directed inwards, we experience our real self (super conscious mind). In meditation, the conscious mind is directed inwards and so people are not aware of anything that is happening around them. This is the highest level of meditation, which is indeed difficult but possible. It is a process by which one can attain unimaginable powers.

Proper Planning

The ability to plan well in advance helps a person in the various tasks he has to perform in his life. The better the plan, the easier it is for him to overcome procrastination. Proper planning helps in saving time. It helps to manage time in an effective manner. When you have a proper plan for your work, your time is not wasted in thinking about what has to be done or what to start with.

Planning helps one to develop a sense of self-confidence. When we find ourselves working progressively in accordance to the plan, it motivates and energizes us. It raises our self-esteem and self-respect. Visible progress pushes us forward and we start looking at ourselves in a very different, positive manner. As we continue to work with our plan, we will feel more and more effective and powerful, more in control of our life. We naturally get motivated to do much more than what we had thought.

When we plan our work in advance, we find it much easier to get going. We move ahead with greater speed and as we progress we find it smooth sailing. As we already know what we have to do next, less time is wasted in thinking about the procedures and therefore, the working efficiency also increases.

Most people in this world have a definite goal but many of them fail to achieve it because they are not able to create the right path to reach to it. Successful as well as unsuccessful people both have knowledge and they work hard in their mission, but the only difference is, that people who succeed, work on the right path, which takes them straight to the doors of success. While the unsuccessful also work hard, they do not make the right efforts in the right direction.

There are thousands of men and women who have the ability but are depressed or are not satisfied with their own selves in spite of their tiring efforts and hard work. This is just because they do not have a proper plan to work upon. They actually do not know the way to succeed. Such people start blaming others for their failures. This is especially so with the teenagers who are often dependent on their parents or other elders. Instead of finding out what went wrong or what was lacking in themselves, they blame others for not helping and encouraging them.

REMEMBER, working in a planned and organized manner leads to success. You need to decide and set a goal and have a proper plan to achieve the goal. You can always demand support and help from elderly, experienced people but you shouldn't be dependent on them. You have no right to blame them when you are not able to succeed. You fail because of your own mistakes. You fail when you are not able to prepare a proper plan and if you have a proper plan, you fail because you do not follow the plan or do not work hard with it.

A man can fail many times, but he isn't a failure until he begins to blame somebody else for his failure.

When a person is not able to complete a piece of

work, the best excuse he can give is, "I didn't have enough time to complete the work." Remember; never say that you do not have time. You have exactly the same number of hours per day that were given to Albert Einstein. All you need is proper planning of your time and of your work.

When a person says that he did have time to do a certain piece of work and yet did not do it, there can be only two possible reasons for it. First; he was not willing to do it and the second; he did not know how the work had to be done. If he does not know how to do it, he can be taught, but if he was not willing to do it than nobody can help him. Remember, time does not stand still for anyone. Once it is gone, it is lost forever. You have to manage your time and use it for your betterment.

Time is life,
If you waste your time, you waste your life.
If you plan your time, you plan your life

Every second of your life is important and you should make the best use of your time by planning it for useful and productive works.

Take the example of a magician who performs her magic shows in different states of various countries. She performs a show every day. Sometimes two or even three and the duration of the show is three hours. She performs her shows eleven months a year. Besides magic, she has a keen interest in computers in which she has completed her diploma at the age of seven. She has even acquired a degree in web engineering at the age of nine. In spite of being a busy magician, she never stops working on her laptop. She is also interested in writing books and gives inspiring and motivating speeches to many schools, colleges and organizations. Taking on the role of counselor, she has treated many people suffering from mental problems: some by conversing with them and a few by hypnotism. She attends her school only to answer her examinations and passes with flying colours. You might wonder as to how this 15-year-old girl can perform her magic shows, work on computers, write books, meet her patients and even achieve a good result in academics without attending school. All this is because this little girl believes in proper planning of her work and time. She plans the smallest detail of her work and always keeps progressing. This is not just an imaginary story, but a reality in the life of Suhani Shah, a student of class 9, who's written the book that you are reading.

Someone said that you should do only one job or piece of work at a time but nobody has ever said that we should do only one job the whole day. We can do as many things as we want to in a day but only by planning our work well, and in advance. Planning makes your work easy and shows you what is to be done first and what follows next.

I am not asking you to work for 24 hours nor am I suggesting that you should give up entertainment and relaxation. All I want to make you understand is that the day must be planned. Your time for relaxation, listening to music, getting close to your near and dear ones or for any other entertainment should also be included in the planning.

You should plan your success and work hard with that plan. By the grace of God, you have two things in common with all the successful people of the world. First, you are the master of a mind similar to theirs. Second, you have twenty-four hours a day just as they have. These two factors have not changed over the ages and will not change in the future either. All successful people had and have these two things in common, and so do you.

"Success is never by chance, it is always by choice."

How you use your time is entirely your choice and that is what makes the difference. There is no difference between you and the other successful people. The only thing is that they have used their time in the most fruitful way. They think about their goals and plan them properly, which helps them to understand what is important and what is to be done first, second and so forth. So, with a firm determination, decide your goal, prepare a plan to achieve the goal, follow the plan, work with the best of your ability and open the doors of success.

"Men never plan to be failures; they simply fail to plan to be successful."

—William A. Ward.

Your plan should be such, that it would make you feel that working with it will definitely make you achieve success. You need to have 100% confidence on your plan, only then your plan will be of some use. If you are not sure that you will achieve success through your plan then the plan is useless. You need to give complete attention to preparing a well-organized plan, after thinking and analyzing the whole matter.

A well-prepared plan smoothens your efforts. When you have a step-by-step process of achieving your goal, you multiply your chances of success. As you journey towards the completion of your task and achieve success, you are fully aware of the things you have to do and how they are to be done. Now it's time for your body to get into action.

Time

"TIME" certainly is the most precious commodity in this world. Although, we all know it, we are not able to understand its value and its need to be used in a proper manner. It is priceless and bows before none. You cannot buy it with the wealth you possess nor can you stop it from passing by. You may have wealth today; tomorrow you might not. Your wealth makes you feel rich, it is only a momentary feeling but as time passes, you never know what is going to happen. You are just a caretaker of whatever you posses. You have to take care of your possessions until you survive. After you, some other person will become the owner of your wealth. It is the present moment that makes you rich, therefore remember, it does not take much time for the moment to change.

You never know, when times will change and you might have to go through a very critical situation in life. It might be the worst situation in your life. There are many people who are going through such a condition even today. If you feel that you are trapped from all sides and find no way to walk on, this is the time when you need to work with courage. Never give up. If you give up you lose the battle against life. You should work courageously with a strong faith in God. Always remember, only after a dark and silent night, arrives the pleasant bright morning sunlight. No power on earth can ever stop this wonderful happening. Likewise if you are experiencing a bad time, do not feel sad or depressed. Be courageous and keep going until the good times knock on your door, for one day they are sure to come.

Well, no person ever changes. What changes is TIME. You will find somebody very kind, somebody who treats you with love and courtesy, somebody who feels and expresses sadness and loneliness when it is time to leave him. However, later on, as time passes you will find the same person does not even recognize you. What you are is not because you wanted to be what you are. It is the time, situations and circumstances that made you as you are and if you find some changes in a person or in yourself, it is due to the time and the conditions that one goes through.

We get to live our life only once and this life span is not very long. We can't even realize how fast time passes. In this entire life span, we can change only one person, and that is our self. So, why not always try to improve the quality of our life by working upon ourselves and the abilities that are within us. Why not always make the best use of the time we have!

Today if you are crying, tomorrow you might not be. We have to learn to walk along with "TIME". Time will never stand still. Likewise, we should not allow life to stand still. Every single moment of life is a learning experience, which can be enjoyed but only if you realize it. Time that has gone by is not going to return. This doesn't mean that you have to sit and worry about the lost time. By doing so, you waste more time. Stop wasting time by utilizing it fruitfully. Time controls life on this earth.

However, those who understand the perfect value of time and experience every second of it, achieve mastery over their own life.

TIME SHOULD NOT BE WASTED

We all know that time is very precious yet; many of us do not use it for fruitful works. Successful people understand the value of time and they make an effort to use it wisely and effectively. It helps to improve the quality of life.

> *"Dost thou love life? Then do not squander time,*
> *for that is the stuff life is made of."*

Many people have got into the habit of wasting time. This is not an inborn habit, but is created by the person himself. Different people waste time in different ways just because they do not make a conscious effort to realize that the activity they are doing is going to help them in no way. You might even have many time-wasters in your daily routine, which you might not be consciously aware of.

Here are a few examples:

- Time is wasted in gossiping, laziness, telephone calls, etc. People enjoy such activities but they do not realize that they are wasting their valuable time. Such things are not going to do any good to them, neither now nor in the future.
- Day dreaming and pondering over unnecessary matters is also a waste of time. We start dreaming or think about something or somebody and just waste our time. By the time we come back to our senses, we realize that our thoughts have been useless. Emotions like love, hatred, jealously, greed, anger, fear or excessive attachments cause us to daydream. Such emotions and feelings have no importance as they have no existence in practical life. They not only waste our

time and distract our mind from the main job but they also decrease our concentration power and our working efficiency. Due to such feelings, we are not able to give our complete attention to the one particular job. They divert our mind and we are then not able to concentrate on what we are doing.

- There are people who waste time in smoking, drinking several cups of tea or coffee or in having snacks or uselessly chatting with people who sit around.
- Some people waste time talking on the telephone. Even after the message is delivered, they chat and gossip over the phone for a long time. Some people have nothing important to discuss but they make a phone call just to pass their time.

As I said, different people waste their time in different ways. Some are aware of it while some are unaware. One must try to understand the value of time in one's life. Try to identify your time wasters and after identifying them, take effective measures to correct them. The best way to get rid of your time wasters is to involve yourself in other beneficial activities that could keep your mind off your time wasters.

If you feel that you are free and have nothing to do, try to relax your mind by meditating or keeping your body and mind fit by performing yoga or certain exercises. You can also get into a habit of reading books: books that could motivate and inspire you. You can complete your pending work or the work that you might have left for some other day. You can also involve yourself in some sports or in artistic work or something that you like so that it could improve you and your abilities. Try to focus on useful matters and avoid your time wasters, as they are your biggest enemies.

"Do not waste any part of your time. Do not allow even a minute to pass without making the best use of it."

TIME MANAGEMENT

Everybody is busy. Adults don't have time to complete all their work while children don't have time to complete their homework. Whether at work or at home, one has to finish many activities within twenty-four hours of the day. In such a scenario, managing time becomes essential and time management has now become very necessary for every human being. Even if some part of our work is not completed on time, we are not able to manage the other jobs of the day.

Time-management is essential for all successful people – this is one of the practical techniques which have helped the leading people in all fields, be it business, sport, entertainment or public service, reach the pinnacles of their careers. It is all about sorting out important and unimportant work and giving time to each work accordingly. It involves using your common sense to use your time in the most effective and productive manner.

Time is the most valuable and priceless element. Once it is lost, you can never retrieve it. Therefore, value this element and try to make the best use of it. Here are a few tips for managing time and using it in the most effective way possible:-

- Sort out what is most important and what is the least important, that can be dropped.
- Use your spare time in the most effective manner. Use it for fruitful works.

- Concentrate on your work and avoid distractions. Stop daydreaming. This wastes time and even decreases working efficiency.
- Avoid procrastination
- Try increasing your working speed. Work energetically and reduce stress.

Use your time in a well-organized way and plan your day properly to avoid time wastage. Time management is a skill that involves planning every second of the hour for productive results. You have not to concentrate on being busy for 24 hours of the day but on the results of the work you are doing. Many people work for days but achieve very little of what they need to. This is because of not concentrating on the right things. Hence, ensure that you concentrate as much of your time and energy as possible on the 'high-returns' tasks so that you achieve the greatest benefit with the limited time available to you.

NOTHING EVER STOPS

Time waits for none, but it can change anything and anyone. Some unfortunate events and incidents leave an impact on our lives. There may be matters that leave you in great grief and distress. However, always REMEMBER, all sorrows, miseries and pain move away with time. No person can carry the same intensity of grief throughout his life. Time is the greatest healer of all. All one needs is to give his mind the time it demands to cure the wounds of the past. Let your sorrows settle down and look towards life in a positive manner and you will soon find that things are improving. Nothing ever stops. **Time, too, constantly moves on**.

"Although life is full of suffering, it is also full of the overcoming of it."

—Helen Keller

Communication Skills

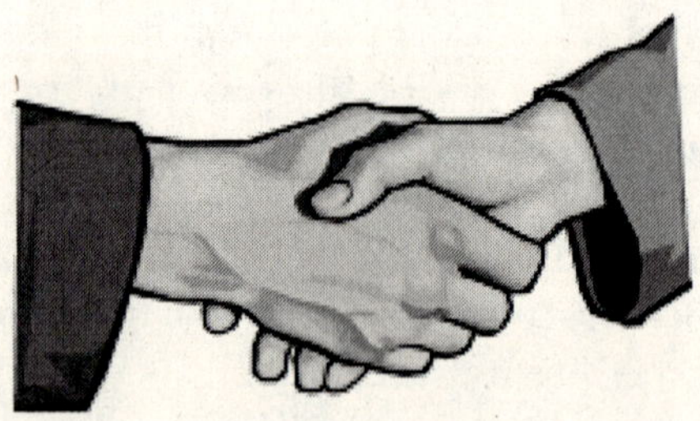

In today's life, being highly educated and having knowledge of all the facts and figures of the particular field in which one is trying to move ahead is not enough for progressing. It is a competitive world. There may be others besides you who are trying their hand in the same field, who are also knowledgeable. However, you should have the confidence to present yourself in an effective and attractive manner. Your manner of communicating and dealing with others makes you win the race.

From a hundred, only very few capable candidates are called for an interview, and from those few capable candidates, just one gets the job. All those who are called, may have the degrees that make them capable for the job but the one who proves himself more smart and has the power to deal with and convince the interviewer, wins the job.

Being a good conversationalist is useful in all walks of life, be it professional or personal. How you greet a person, how you talk, what you speak and how you leave. All these reflect your nature and show your level of confidence.

Talking to people skillfully determines the quality of your life, whether in business, family or your social life.

Does a handshake really make a difference?

Well, the person with a high level of confidence will always greet the person he meets with a stiff and firm handshake. YES, it certainly attracts and makes an impression on the other person. Your handshake easily describes your mood and your interest. A light and loose one says that you are either tired or you are not interested in the person or in the matter to be discussed. Such a handshake decreases the enthusiasm of the other person. On the contrary, your energy and interest in the other person seems to be really good when you greet someone with a nice firm handshake. You appear fresh and energetic and this delights the other person too. Our confidence level is easily seen and you leave having created a good impression. Therefore, all those of you who usually just stand up and say "HI" or "HELLO" on meeting a person and "BYE" or "THANK YOU" on leaving, do add a nice handshake. That helps communication and adds to your personality.

This is about how you greet people. This makes the first impression and the last. Though the appearance and confidence is good, the main matter will be discovered when you speak. The food might look delicious, but it's of no use if it's really not so, when tasted.

The first and basic rule to be understood is: People are 99.9% interested in themselves and only the remaining part, in you. Many amongst us are not effective in dealing with others because we constantly keep thinking and talking about ourselves. To become a good conversationalist, you need to first try and understand people and their nature. Understanding people and their nature simply as means to know what they are and realize that they are not always like the way you think they are or what you want them to be.

For a better and effective start, try to pick the subject that interests the other person the most. If you do not know much about the other person, let me help you out. For any person, the most interesting topic to talk about is the person himself. When you talk to others about themselves, they will be deeply interested in you and will like you for doing so. Ask them about their health, their family, about business or anything that relates to them. Always REMEMBER, it is not about how you like what you speak; instead, it is about how your listeners find it.

Nevertheless, when you are involved in a professional or formal conversation, then just speaking about matters off the main point is useless. Therefore, in such cases, quickly get to the main point and try to explain what you want to in a clear and understandable manner.

Always try to be very specific in whatever you say. Speaking more than required is useless. It may be better

to speak less. If your views are being liked, you will be asked to say more and if not, then nothing will make a difference.

Many people waste a lot of time getting to the point. They are not able to properly explain what they actually want to say. They keep on rattling around the subject instead of getting to the main matter. This actually bores the listeners, makes them impatient and finally, frustrated. Giving the most importance to the main point and quickly getting to the point is a very valuable skill in business. Many people are known and remembered for their way of communicating. When you are in a professional or formal conversation, there are certain points that should be taken into consideration while talking, if you want people to take interest in you or in your talks or in both.

The point that you put forward should be absolutely clear in your mind and you should be able to answer any question regarding the matter. It is your duty to place your views and ideas before people in such a manner that they can clearly understand them and, if good, then even appreciate them.

One always likes to listen to the person who listens and takes interest in what one has to say. Therefore, always keep your attention on the person you are talking to, as a person will not get interested in your talk if you do not get interested in his.

When a person is talking, he expects your total interest in his talks and if he does not find it, he loses his interest in conversing with you. Hence, if you wish to have a healthy conversation, always look at the other person. Question him when you are not able to understand some points and keep nodding your head when you do. On receiving a good response, the other person becomes more free and comfortable with you as he finds that you are able to understand him in a proper manner. If he likes to talk and discuss with you, he will also like to work with you.

The number of listeners in this world is almost half the number of speakers. It is a fast moving world. People do not have time to know much about others and listen to what the other person wants to say. They just want people to listen to them. Therefore, when somebody finds such a person who is ready to listen and even understand him, then his interest in the person increases. Therefore, always listen to the other person and let him complete what he is saying. Stopping him in between is a sign of domination or behaviour indicating avoidance.

Eye Patterns

When you are in a conversation, the movements of your eyes certainly make a difference. The other person is not aware of what is going on in your mind. He always expects that when he is talking to you, you should look at him because it shows that you are interested in what he has to say and are visibly listening to what he has to say. Eye movement patterns reflect what is going on in one's mind.

- If the eyes are just moving here and there and not at the one who is speaking, it easily reflects that the person is not interested in listening and is waiting for the other person to finish. It could also be that he is looking at somebody or something beside him.
- When one is constantly looking at one particular point but not at the speaker, it says that though he is there, his mind is somewhere else. There is some other matter that is actually rotating in the person's mind.

- When one is looking at the speaker and responding, it states that one is consciously listening to him.
- When another person is speaking and one is playing with some other thing- it could be his cell phone, his pen or something else it irritates and can even frustrate the other person. He correctly guesses that the person's concentration is divided. You cannot totally concentrate on two things at one particular time.

These points might not always be exactly as explained but the situations may be similar. Along with the eye patterns, noticing the other person's mood and behaviour is important as you get to know whether he is really interested in your matter or not.

Always treat the other person as you wish to be treated.

One always likes to hear something positive about oneself. When talking with somebody, try to notice some of his good qualities or his appearance. Mention it to him after having finished your discussion on the main matter. This makes the other person feel good and happy. However, one thing must be kept in mind; that whatever you speak should be true enough for the other person to believe. Otherwise, instead of being happy, he will feel that you are trying to flatter him for your purpose or are making fun of him. This can make right things go wrong.

Example:
Robin went for an interview and asked for permission to meet Mr. George, the boss. The employee present there told him that Mr. George was busy.

Robin: "Could you please try and ask him to see me for 5 minutes. He told me to meet him at this time. He might have forgotten".

Employee: "Sorry sir. I cannot help you. We have been ordered not to disturb him."

Robin: "Okay, I shall try some other day. Anyway,

you seem to be very good at your work. However, if you just have a little smile on your face, you will look even better".

The employee had a few spots on his face, was quite short in height and was receiving such a compliment for the first time. It was hard for him to accept it. He first thought that Robin was making fun of him. Robin understood this and before the employee could say anything, Robin added,

"Excuse me sir. Do not get me wrong. I think no one has ever noticed your smile, not even you. You honestly look good.

The employee who had always focused on his weak points was happy to receive such a compliment.

Employee: "Thanks for the compliment and your notification. The boss is busy right now, therefore, you can come tomorrow at 4pm and I shall make it convenient for you to meet Mr. George".

Making the other person feel good is the first step towards influencing him.

To be a good speaker, it is important for you to make your listeners feel good.

Whenever involved in a conversation, be it formal or casual, making the other person feel good means half your work is done. The best way to make any person feel good is to make him feel important. Never neglect the other person. He is equally important to himself as you are to yourself. Therefore, when they see that they are important to you, they feel good. You need not tell them directly that they are important but your words and actions should reflect it.

- Listen to them
- Do not interrupt while they speak, let them complete whatever they have to say
- Use their names while talking to them

- Compliment them when they deserve it

When you give importance to them, they feel honoured; they like you for your attention to them and they respond to you very well.

> ***The best conversationalist will always talk from his conscious mind and will remember that it is not obvious for him to always be right.***

When you are discussing a matter, if you stick to your point and do not make a conscious effort to listen and understand what the other person has to say, then you will always find him wrong. Hence, listen to people, agree with them if you find them right and help them understand your view if you find them wrong. It is easiest to disagree with people. Every silly person can do it. But it takes a sensible man to agree. Whenever you find the other person right, let him know that you agree with him. Nod your head with a 'YES' or tell the person that you agree with him or say, "You are right". Such words delight the other person and he shall find you humble and understanding and shall feel good about working with you or for you.

When you disagree with the other person, try to clearly explain him your view. It is good if he understands but if he does not then gradually leave the matter: change the subject. Let him not know that you actually disagree with him unless necessary. When he realizes that you disagree with his views and ideas, he will not like it and he will not like you for disagreeing with him. Hence, leave the matter before it turns into an argument. Arguments are for weak people. No person can win an argument as both sides stick to their own points without listening to what the other person has to say. Argument is nothing but a waste of time.

Everybody tries to find his own profit in any deal: it is obvious. Therefore, whenever we want to get something done, show the other person what his benefit is, in doing the work. Everything is done for a reason. Give him a reason to do the work. The reason should benefit him and allow him to do the work satisfactorily. Try to avoid showing him your benefit in getting the work done. When the other person looks at your benefit, he might lose focus of his own advantage. No one will like some other person to get the benefit of the work that has been done by him. Thus, show them their benefit and not yours. Make them realize what they stand to gain or lose by accepting or denying the deal.

Some people are masters in receiving a positive reply. It's not because they are lucky or have some special powers but they certainly have the quality of making the other person say what they want them to. It is a skill that can be learned.

Whenever you want the other person to say a "YES" to you, talk to them and question them in such a manner that the only answer they can give is a "YES". To get a positive response from the other person, you first need to get the person into a positive state of mind.

Example: You work at a designer show room and wish to sell a dress to a lady. So, before you get to the dress, get the lady in a positive state by setting her a few questions.

- "You wish to buy a good dress madam, don't you?"

The answer in her mind is 'YES'

- "You want the best value for your money, don't you?"
  She certainly does.

Asking such questions sets the person's mind in a positive state. The lady now feels that you are going to show her nothing but the best. The chance of your receiving an affirmative answer increases.

Besides this, supply choices to the other person. When you give them alternatives, they will think about the other when they are not satisfied with one. Keep this basic point in mind that we are not interested in receiving a negative answer. Even when you place options before the other person, both the options should be in your favour.

- "Shall I start work from tomorrow or Monday?"

In any case, you are starting on your job.

- "Shall I shall meet you this evening or tomorrow at noon?"

It could be anytime, but you are receiving an appointment.

- "Do you wish to buy the black one or shall I pack the white one for you?"

It is better to ask this instead of, "Do you wish to purchase one of these?"

This might not work at all times but it will most of the time.

The purpose of communication skills is to deliver your message to others in the best way possible. By successfully getting your message across, you convey your thoughts and ideas effectively. It is about how you get your work done and leave a good impression on others just by what you speak. Your talking represents your thoughts. It shows your confidence, your maturity and your ability to understand what the other person is demanding from you. Having better communication skills helps a person to be better in presenting himself, being confident and most importantly, winning others just by words, in both business and personal life.

Decision-Making

Our future is like a piece of blank paper waiting to be written on. We can write a story describing the most wonderful and fulfilling life on it but in order to create such a bright future and make the necessary changes, we first need to know what we are, what we want and what is the right path to achieve it.

There is only one person who knows everything about you: what is right for you and what is not, whether whatever you are doing is worth the effort or isn't, or even if you need to change or not and that person is YOU. You are the only one who knows everything about you. Therefore, realizing your inner self and abilities and knowing where you are NOW is very important before you step forward. If you wish to make any changes or take certain decisions, you should first make up your mind about them and satisfy your inner self in such a way that no other person or happenings can change your thoughts.

Making proper decisions at the proper time and staying with them without getting into any dilemma is the quality of decision-making and is very necessary to lead a proper life. Very often, we reach a point in our life where there are two roads and we have to choose one of them to walk on. We get confused and are not able to select the right path. The ability to take proper and correct decisions at the proper time is very important for every person, child or adult. It is necessary because one should be able to decide and understand what is right for him and what is not. This quality is needed at every moment of your life.

When you start taking your own decisions, you become independent. This is the only quality by which you prepare yourself to face various challenges of life. You might be wrong at times but this does not mean that you can never do it.

Never be in a confused state of mind. Whatever the matter may be, sit down calmly, give it a thought and take the right decision. Once you take a decision, then remain steady with it. Don't keep changing your mind. After the right decision has been taken, then thinking of the other choice is just foolishness and a waste of time. Don't go for any other choice thereafter.

Initially, when you start taking your own decisions, you may sometimes make mistakes. Try to learn from them. Understand the reason behind your incorrect decision. After making a few mistakes, you will gradually learn to take the right decisions.

Therefore, start taking your own decisions from now. The earlier you start, the earlier you'll prepare yourself to face different challenges of life.

Start now, even if at times you fail to take the correct decisions, your practice and different experiences will be a great teacher.

Decisions should not be taken on the basis of emotions. When we are carried away by emotions, we don't think about what is right and what's wrong. Emotions are not steady. They can change but your mind never changes. The mind is always the same. If such decisions are made then the emotional talks or deeds that were the basis for your decision may change any time and prove your decision wrong. When decisions are influenced by one's emotions, then one usually has to suffer in the future.

All decisions should be made by the conscious mind. One's conscious mind can think properly upon matters and can generate proper and correct decisions. The subconscious mind can be right but not always. If somebody or something influences the subconscious mind then the decision may be wrong.

The ability of decision-making is very important for any person but more important than decision-making is trying to understand the effect of each decision. No decision should be made just to complete a job. Often many other people are affected by our decisions. It could be decisions regarding the matters of the company, family or friends. Therefore, if one is not serious about his own decisions, then others also will not be. It is very necessary to value and respect your decisions.

Not much time should be wasted in taking decisions. Decisions must be taken after analyzing the complete matter and thinking upon it properly but after this work is over then we should not waste time in its implementation. If proper decisions are not made at the proper time then they have no value.

A boy sees a wrist watch in a shop. He finds it a bit costly. He is willing to buy it but does not have sufficient money. He goes home and keeps thinking about the watch and whether he should buy it or not. After pondering over it for two days, he finally decides to buy the watch. He borrows money from his friends and goes to the shop but finds that the watch is not there! It was sold to some other person the previous day Therefore, decisions have no value if they are not made at the proper time. Decision-making is not a matter to be postponed.

Decisions should not be made under any sort of fear or bias. They should not be based on prejudice. Personal emotions and feelings must be kept aside while making a decision. Decisions should be made after proper understanding of the matter and its implementation should also be at the right time.

Hard Work

In a small town of India, a lottery business was established and booths were opened at many places. All of them were making a roaring business. The lucky number was being announced in the afternoon and the person with that number used to get a hundred times the money he paid for his lottery ticket. Many people got interested in buying such tickets. Instead of earning their livelihood by doing their jobs, they used to hang around these lottery booths and try their luck everyday. They used to think that one day they would win a lottery and become rich overnight. Those lottery counters collected a large amount from the poor workers of the town everyday. As a result of this, many homes were ruined, many men committed suicide and this state of affairs continued until this lottery business was banned in the entire state by the High Court.

This is just an example to explain that nothing can be gained without hard work. Nobody can give you what you want, if you are not ready to pay for it.

Lazy people believe in fate while wise people believe in action. Where there is action, there is surely a reaction.

Many people try to become rich in a day; they aspire for comforts without working for them. They desire great things but are not ready to work for them. They simply want all their desires to be served to them on a silver plate. If becoming rich is your aim, then work for it. If you work you are going to get something and this something might someday become everything.

"The road to success has no short cuts. It has no other route except that of hard labour."

Nobody has ever achieved success without hard work. Success is not something that you can get by luck. It demands a lot of preparation and hard work and it is a fact that the harder you work the luckier you get. The harder a person works, the better he feels and the better he feels, the harder he works. Without hard work, there is no success. You cannot learn how to spell just by sitting with a dictionary. Everything that we enjoy is the result of someone's hard work. Some work is visible while some goes unseen, but both are equally important. The best artists practice for three months just to perform a three-hour show. We should also learn from nature. The duck keeps paddling relentlessly underneath but appears smooth and calm on top. Michaelangelo once said, "If people knew how hard I had to work to gain my mastery, it wouldn't seem wonderful at all."

Excellence is not luck; it is the result of a lot of hard work and practice. It also demands many sacrifices. Remember, hard work and practice makes a person better at whatever he is doing.

"Success is a failure kicked to pieces by hard-work."

There is no magic wand for success. In reality success

comes to doers and not to dreamers. Nature gives birds their food but does not put it into their nest. They have to work hard to get it. Nothing comes easy. The best musicians practice everyday and so they are the best. The horse that pulls the carriage never kicks and a horse that kicks never pulls. So, stop kicking and start pulling.

All successful people through all time reached their particular success by labouring for it.

No one has ever got to the top without hard work. This is a recipe. It might not always take you to the top, but will definitely get you pretty near.

There was an actor whose films were very popular. His name was written on the hearts of the audience. But every year when he attended the award shows, he returned empty handed. However, it never disappointed him. His determination and love for his work was never affected. Once his child asked him, "Daddy, you act so well, still you don't get any award. This is not fair." He replied to his child in a very polite manner, "My child, I work hard for each of my shots and try to put in my very best. If the audience thinks that I deserve an award I will definitely get it someday. I don't need to demand it." He kept on working harder and harder, not for the award but for himself.

At last, at the age of sixty-two he attended his last award show on a wheel chair. All his life he had worked incredibly hard and this time he was surprised to hear his own name for the 'Lifetime Achievement Award'. When he was taken onto the stage, he asked for the microphone and looking at his son, said, "Look my child, I haven't demanded it, I have earned it."

This is to explain that your hard work is definitely going to take you somewhere. When you work, you should work for yourself and not for the achievements. If you deserve something, you will get it, but if you do not deserve it, no power on earth can give it to you.

Remember, you should do your work with full concentration and complete confidence. Do not think of what you are going to get in return for your work. Do your work for your inner happiness and satisfaction.

Thou has a right only on your actions,
Thou has no right on the fruits of those actions.
Do all actions without attachment or motive,
The fruit of action should not be thy motive.
Do your work in a spirit of great sacrifice,
Perform your duty without attachment or price.
Craving and anger impel to do the sins,
Those who have gained wisdom can avoid those sins.
— Bhagavad-Gita

"Vices get punishment and virtues get reward,
Sooner or later everybody gets his due award."

Work harder and harder and harder and you are getting closer and closer to success.

Always stay happy and enjoy the work you do. Do it to the best of your ability. Don't think about what you are going to get in return. REMEMBER, as you sow, so shall you reap. If you have really worked hard then you are definitely going to get what you deserve. Do your work for your inner happiness and after it is done, your duty is over. Now, you should get ready for the next task without waiting for the results. If you have confidence that you have worked hard and with complete honesty then you should also be confident of its results. Therefore, never wait for fruits; if you deserve them then you will get them, if not today then tomorrow or day after, but definitely someday.

Do not feel that your family background doesn't allow you to do what you have decided, or your financial condition is not as good as you need in order to achieve your goal. Always remember; where there is a will, there is a way. Just decide your goal and be steady with it. Have the confidence to achieve your goal. Prepare a clear and a proper plan of how are you going to achieve it. Concentrate only on your goal, leaving everything else aside and lastly, work as hard as you can to achieve your goal. Finally, see all your dreams come true.

Be in a Relaxed State of Mind

Relaxing means to be calm and cool, leaving all tensions and worries aside. It is not just sleeping on the bed or listening to soft music and doing nothing. You can relax yourself even while you are doing some work. While working, you can relax mentally.

We continuously keep working with complete interest in our work for 8 to 10 hours, but after that, we find ourselves getting tired. Well, remember, our brain is like a machine which works as long as we want it to. It is tireless. So, what makes us feel tired?

There can be many answers.

- Maybe we are bored doing the same kind of work for a long time. This gradually decreases our working efficiency and we lose interest in it.
- We are in a hurry to get back home or to attend to some other work.
- Sometimes, we are carried away by emotions like

anxiety, love, jealously, anger, etc. that divert our mind from our work and as a result we do not feel interested in doing the work.

- While working if we start thinking about the past happenings or some unhappy incidents, we lose concentration in the work.

Whatever work we are doing, the most necessary thing is to do it with a cool and relaxed mind. Only then can we concentrate on our work and do it in the most effective manner. If our mind is not calm then it will keep evolving on different matters and we will have no interest in doing the work that we are actually supposed to. No work can be done properly if it is not done with complete interest. Therefore, try to keep your mind cool, calm and relaxed while working.

Mr. George worked in a chemical factory. He had a tough job. The job was tough because he had a very malicious boss. His boss never missed a chance to dominate over him and find fault with him. The boss never allowed him to work with a calm mind. On his way back home, Mr. George used to think about the happenings at the factory that always troubled him. At home, he would shout at his wife on finding his tea cold, scold his little child who asked him for something and quarreled with the neighbours whose music system blared loudly.

There was nothing wrong with Mr. George. The only problem was that he was not in a relaxed state of mind.

To be in a relaxed state of mind, you need to let go things that are not very important, without paying much attention to them.

Whenever somebody or something disturbs you, your mind suddenly gets upset. Even when you are doing some work with complete concentration, thinking about some matter, reading a book or something else, if your concentration is broken by any happening or by some person, your mind suddenly gets disturbed. When we have a lot of tension, we lose interest in all other matters. Our tensions keep nagging us all the time. When our mind is worked up, it then starts behaving in a queer manner. We start getting angry with people for no reason; we start acting foolishly and we present ourselves in a very awkward manner. Our whole personality begins to change. All this is just because our mind is not in a relaxed state. Therefore, it is very necessary to be cool, calm and relaxed while working.

Relaxation is very necessary. Your mind keeps thinking about different matters and your body keeps working. Some people say that they have to do lot of work in a day and it is not possible for them to relax and sleep in the afternoons. Well, relaxation does not mean only sleeping. You can relax even while working. There are different ways to relax your mind and body even while working.

You can play soft music in the background while working. This may keep you fresh and help you work energetically. However, if you feel that you are being disturbed by the music or the music is diverting your concentration from your work then switch it off.

You can take a break for about 5 to 10 minutes in between and perform certain breathing exercises. There are many books available in the market regarding such exercises. Here are two exercises.

- Sit down on a chair in an erect posture. Keep your hands on your lap and close your eyes. Calm your mind and try to forget everything that is bothering you. Take a deep breath as slowly as you can. Let your chest be filled with fresh air. After breathing in fully, hold your breath for a few seconds and exhale. Do not throw out your breath all at once. Exhaling should be slow, as slow as you can manage. While inhaling, you should feel that the air is going through your whole body. You should feel your body being filled with love, strength, purity, honesty, knowledge and courage. While exhaling you should feel that your body is eliminating all its impurities, jealousy, anger, hatred and fatigue. Keep repeating this process of inhaling and exhaling for about five to ten times, according to the availability of time. After you finish this exercise, rub your hands against each other and move them touching your face. Slowly open your eyes, stand and get back to work. You will feel fresh, energetic and even relaxed.

- While working if you have an argument or get angry with somebody then your mind gets disturbed. The best way to relax at that very moment is to close your eyes and slowly count up to 10. You will find it difficult when you start and reach up to 5 and 6 because when you are angry and your mind is totally disturbed, you will never like to count. However, count till 10, rub you hands against each other, move them over your face and slowly open your eyes. You will again become as normal as you were before you got angry. You will feel fresh and relaxed.

Therefore, be cool, calm and relaxed and enjoy each moment of your life to its fullest.

Age is no bar

In this huge world, each and every person has some power or talent within. One needs to realize and understand that hidden talent. The earlier one recognizes his talent, the easier it becomes for him to use it and even to plan his career. All we need is to decide a goal in life, and concentrate on it. In order to have confidence in ourselves we need to believe in ourselves. We can achieve anything that we think we can. Our age is no bar to accomplish any task in life. Children sometimes think that they are too small and cannot do the things that older people do. This is absolutely wrong. A person of any age can do anything that he wishes to; all one needs is to have the will to do it. Secondly, one needs to give the amount of time, concentration and hard work that the work demands. No task says that you need to be of a certain age to accomplish it.

When people talk about matters concerning career plans, some of them literally have no interest in it. They feel that they are too young and there is a lot of time for them to think about their careers. Well, a career is something that may start early in life, if you think about it at an early age. Therefore, never think that you need to be of a certain age to decide your career. A child, a teenager or an adult, all have their future, which needs to be filled with bright colours, and this lies entirely in their hands. One should never feel that the time to do something is gone or yet to come. Your future is yet to come and so do whatever you wish without bothering about your age.

A study of the mind has proved that in a person's life, his mind works most powerfully between the ages of two and nine years. His observation and grasping power is at its peak during this age. Therefore, it should never be said that children have no mind. Children have a mind but they lack in experience and proper understanding. Children should never be ignored. On the contrary, they should be supported and encouraged. You must have heard about many wonder children. The only wonder in those children is that they realized and understood their inner talent and worked hard to develop it. We should remember that each one of us has a certain power or talent within. We should realize it and work upon it without giving an excuse of age. Your age makes no difference. If there is something that makes a difference then it is your mind. If your mind says that you can do something then just go for it. Your mind has all the power. Everything depends on the development of one's mind. The mind of a 10 year old child can be better than that of a 20 year old. Therefore, recognizing a person's ability by his age is not right.

Some people come to a certain age and stop progressing. They feel that their time is now over. They feel that they have done many things and accomplished many tasks. They think that it is now their time to rest. REMEMBER, the time to rest is when you don't actually have the time for it. When you feel that you have done many things and you are getting older, look towards life with a positive attitude and with a feeling of doing and accomplishing some new tasks. You will definitely get something out of it.

Your age makes no difference. Age is just related to the physical growth of the body and not to the development of mind. A child can be much more confident than an older person while the mind of an old person can be much more fresh and energetic than that of a teenager. Therefore, everything is dependent on one's mind. Age makes no difference. Therefore, stop thinking about your age and keep improving your mind and your abilities, for that is what makes all the difference.

Mistakes

Nobody willingly commits a mistake; mistakes are just the wrong decisions that are taken in haste. It is a fact that every human being commits mistakes. "I never make mistakes." Keeping this thought in mind is also a mistake.

A mistake is never big or small. A mistake is a mistake. Thinking of it as big or small is just for one's satisfaction.

We always try to find fault with others but we should never forget that in this huge world no one is perfect. Therefore, before looking for faults in others we should first try to find them in ourself because looking for faults in others before looking for them in ourself is also a mistake.

Before getting angry at the mistakes made by others, one should always remember one's own mistakes"

The best teachers in this world are our mistakes.

Therefore, we should always learn from them and try not to repeat them. No teacher can teach you the practical principles of life, which you can learn from your own mistakes. The only thing most of us try to learn from our mistakes is how to blame others for it. It is said that **a guilty mind always suspects others**. By putting the blame of your mistakes on others, you are trying to cover up your mistakes, which is also a mistake. Therefore, the best thing is to admit the mistake because a person's character is always judged by the book he reads, the company he keeps and the mistakes he admits.

"There is no greater courage than that of recognizing one's own mistakes."

Many people are afraid of the punishment and so they do not admit to having made the mistake. They just ignore it.

We can do three things with our mistakes:

- Refuse to admit them
- Ignore them
- Admit and learn from them

In admitting your mistake, you need to be very brave and courageous. It is really risky but rewarding. Wise people learn from their mistakes while wiser people learn from other people's mistakes. Our life is not long enough for us to learn only from our mistakes.

Remember again, friends, as you sow so shall you reap. If you have committed a mistake then you will definitely have to pay for it. Therefore, it is better to admit the mistake and at least satisfy yourself by improving upon it.

A famous pianist once said that if he played all the notes correctly then nobody would notice him, but if he played just one note incorrectly, then every single person would notice him. This is human nature. A mistake seems to attract the attention of all, more than the dozens of things that go on smoothly.

Many people just ruin their day by brooding and being disappointed over their mistakes. They forget the many things they did that went well and concentrate on the things that went wrong. They don't look at themselves in a positive way and the ego in them always keeps pinching them over their imperfection.

Once we realize and learn from our mistakes then we can do ourselves a favour by putting them out of our mind and concentrating on what went well. This would be a simple and gentle way to face ourselves and end our day with peace and lots of confidence for the coming bright, new day.

"The sages do not consider that making no mistake is a blessing. They believe, rather, that the great virtue of man lies in his ability to correct his mistakes and continually to make a new man of himself."

—Wang Yang-Ming

Make Your Troubles, Your Blessings

In our lives, we usually keep thinking about the things we do not have. We always think 'if I had this' or 'if I had that'. We have many desires and wishes which we want to fulfill. Well, life is all about making your wishes come true. Just sit down for a while and imagine what would happen if we had everything that we desired. There would be nothing for us to look forward to. We feel that if we owned everything that we could think of then our life would become fantastic. It would be simply wonderful. But wait... THINK AGAIN... instead of being wonderful, it would rather become miserable. We lead our lives to make our wishes come true, but if we already have everything that we wish for, then we would lose the charm of our life. We would then have no dreams, no desires and no wishes. Therefore, instead of being sad or depressed, we should rather be happy about what we have and even for what we don't have. For the things that we do not own have given us a chance to look forward to achieving something in life and to filling our lives with excitement, challenges and rewards.

Every person faces troubles and problems in life but only a few succeed in handling and managing them in a proper and effective manner. You should never get worried or depressed when you are facing a problem. On the contrary, you should be thankful to God for problems in life as these problems give us a chance to grow. Try to have a positive approach for every setback in your life.

- If you make a mistake, never give up. It has given you a chance to improve your abilities. Be happy for it teaches you valuable lessons of life.
- Face every new challenge in life with enthusiasm, for it will help you to lead a fearless life and build up your strength, character and personality.
- When you do not know something or you are unaware of something, be happy, it gives you the opportunity to keep learning and keep progressing in life.
- Be happy for the bad and difficult times of your life; those critical moments give you the opportunity to grow and be a better and stronger person in the future.
- Be happy when you are tired and exhausted, because this is the only time that helps you to realize that you have made an effort.

We are always happy and thankful to God for the good things and for the happy moments He gave us, but along with it, we should be much more thankful to Him for the setbacks in our lives as only after experiencing a dark and silent night, can we understand the charm of the pleasant morning sunlight. Therefore, to lead a life of rich fulfillment, try to have a positive outlook towards every negative thing in life. Be thankful for the happy and joyful moments as well as for setbacks, as they maintain the balance of your life. REMEMBER, gratitude can turn a negative into a positive. Always try to be happy and thankful to God for your troubles and you will make them your blessings.

Here is a true story of a boy named Thomas. Thomas was from a middle class family, whose mother died when he was just 16. He had two younger brothers and a sister. His father died when he was 18, leaving nothing but some debts and the burden of younger brothers and a sister on his small shoulders. Thomas himself wanted to complete his studies and become a successful doctor. His relatives told him to distribute his brothers and sister among them so that it would be better for him and his future. Thomas immediately refused as he knew that his relatives would treat them no better than slaves. People told him that he would not be able to take up the responsibility of his brothers and sister properly. They said that it would be enough if he made a happy living at least for himself. Thomas answered them, "I know what I am doing and I have already planned my future. You people do not need to worry about us." Thomas's words surprised people and they then felt that it was no use talking to him. At last, they told Thomas, "Do whatever you wish to, but as time passes, your resolve will become weak and you will not be able to carry on any more, then you will understand what life is all about and realize your mistake. At that moment, please do not give away your life." Thomas heard them and ignored what they said. From that time onwards, Thomas with a firm determination to complete his task, prepared a complete plan to achieve his goal. He found a job, which brought him a good amount of money and he managed his family and studies within his earnings. He believed that there is no gain without pain. He never lost faith and his decisions were never found to be weak. His confidence and a positive attitude helped him to get through all the difficulties that life presented to him. After some years, it was found that young Thomas was now Dr. Thomas De Souza; his brothers were studying in the Central High School and his sister was in a girls' school. When he was asked about how he was able to cope the debts and make a successful and happy living, he replied, "My dad always taught me one thing which I never forgot. I believe that nothing in this world is impossible and every problem has a solution. Instead of focusing on the problem I tried to focus on the solution. I wrote down in a book what I wanted to do and how I wanted to do it. Every morning when I woke up, I used to read it so that my mind was not diverted towards any other useless thing. The more I read it, the way to achieve it seemed easier."

Therefore, start now. Take up a pen and a book. Decide your goal. Write it down in your book, clearly. The destination can never be reached if the road is not clear. Next, write down your plan. It should be a neat, clear and a well-organized plan about which you should be convinced, so that working with it will definitely take you to your goal. You need not take a lifetime just to achieve that one goal. Therefore, next, you should write the time required to complete the task. Time is the most precious commodity in the world. So, when the goal is decided and the plan is prepared, then time should not be wasted in its implementation. Therefore, when you keep reading that you have to achieve your goal in a specific period of time, you do not waste your time in other unnecessary work.

You should often ask three important questions to yourself.

1. What is my goal?
2. How am I going to achieve it? OR
   What is my plan to achieve it?
3. By what time I have to achieve it?

Try asking these questions to yourself right now. If you get the answers then without wasting time, take up a pen and a book and write them down. If you don't get the answers, then sit down quietly, keep your mind cool and calm and think over it. When you get the answers, write them down. REMEMBER, until they are written down they are merely desires; after they are written, they are commitments. Every morning, read it at least once so that it keeps reminding you what your mission is, how and when you have to achieve it. Read it every morning until you achieve your goal. Once you have succeeded, take up another goal in your life and start your journey towards achieving it. GOOD LUCK.

Encouragement

Encouragement is just an act of giving support, courage and hope to the one who needs it. It is an act of persuading somebody to do something by making him realize that he has the ability to do the task.

There should be nothing in the world that can discourage you. It is a fact, that encouragement always helps a person to move ahead in life. However, it is never a necessity. If you fail in your task or you are not able to do something perfectly then you can never give the excuse that there wasn't anybody to encourage you.

You need encouragement when you are not confident about yourself. It is for those people who are weak and feel that they are not capable of doing something. It is for those who have wishes, who see dreams, but do not have the strength, power, confidence and courage to make those dreams come true. Encouragement is to help a person who has talent and who knows where he should go but does not have sufficient amount of self-assurance. It is for those who always think that they can do nothing without the help of others.

You do not need any sort of encouragement if you are confident, determined and courageous. If you think, you can do something then just go for it. If you wait for somebody to come and encourage or support you then there will never be a proper beginning and you'll be wasting your time. Once you start on your way then help and support come automatically. When people will find you progressing, they will on their own come and encourage you. Therefore, never get depressed or disheartened if you find yourself alone on your path. REMEMBER, if there is nobody to encourage you now, there is nothing to worry about because after you achieve your task, you will definitely have at least a few people to do so.

Compete with Yourself

Many people in this world want to be more successful or better than some other person. Everybody wants to be at the top position in his or her respective field and to reach the top they compete with others. They start thinking of themselves as if in a competition with others. They try to be better than others. In one sense, competition is very good but instead of competing with others, one should compete with oneself. When we compete with some other person our progress gets a limit but when we compete with ourselves, the sky is the limit. Instead, of trying to be better than others, try to be better than what you are. You have to compete with yourself and no other person. A singer should and always will try to sing better than before. An artist will always try to perform better than in his previous performance. We should always try to be better than ourselves. When you decide to become like or better than some other person, your progress ends when your task is fulfilled. However, when you want to be better than yourself, then your progress is never-ending.

When you are content to be simply yourself and don't compare or compete, everybody will respect you.

— *Lao Tzu*

You enter a competition when you are not able to recognize yourself or do not have faith in yourself. You compete with others when you find it difficult to define your own worth. You compete when you have a fear of testing yourself.

REMEMBER, it is always easier to beat another person than to do your best. However, these easy and simple ways can make you feel happy for a few moments. Once you win against one person, you will feel very happy for a while, but later you will again find another competitor. So, to be the best, forget about the whole world and be yourself.

You can keep improving yourself at every step. However, for that, you don't need to be better than others. Let others do what they want to and you do what you want to. Success is never-ending and so if you always try to be better than yourself, then even your success will have no end.

Do not Compare

Everybody in this world has unique abilities. Some qualities that you might have, others might not, and vice versa. Therefore, it is no use comparing yourself with others. Remember, the grass on the other side always looks greener. Do not compare yourself with anybody in this world. Be yourself. By comparing yourself with some other person, you are either trying to feel superior to the other person or making the other person superior to you. Do what you want without thinking about anybody else. REMEMBER, that you are the only one in this world. There is nobody like you.

The Beginning...

People have dreams and desires. Dreams remain dreams until they are put into action. If we want to do something, we first need to begin. To reach a destination, we first need to get on the path. Just thinking about the destination will not help us to reach it. Once we get onto the path it becomes easy for us to keep going. When there is work to be done, many people just keep thinking about how to do it. At the same time, there are others who start planning and get into action. Nothing is impossible although it is sometimes difficult. Instead of thinking, one must just start with the work.

"Well begun is half done"

After going through the entire book, I am sure that many of your problems must have been solved. All the abilities that are needed in a person to lead a proper life have been clearly explained in the book. The aim of this book was to guide you by explaining these things to you, but you are really your own greatest helper. After gaining knowledge about so many topics it is now your job to begin. Don't just keep all your good thoughts in your mind but implement them in your day-to-day life. Negative things are easy to work on and will always exert a pull on you. However, even though you may find it easy to start making changes, your path may be filled with great difficulties later on. The positive path can be difficult to walk on, but it will get you to the perfect destination. How to begin is entirely your choice.

GOOD LUCK

"If this book has brought even a slight change in you then my task is accomplished."

—Suhani Shah